A Basic Catholic Dictionary

Alan Griffiths is a priest of the Portsmouth Catholic Diocese and was ordained in 1974. He serves as Parish Priest of Ringwood in Hampshire and has worked for several Committees of the Roman Catholic Bishop's Conference of England and Wales. His last book, *We Give You Thanks And Praise – The Ambrosian Eucharistic Prefaces* – was published by the Canterbury Press in 1999.

Other titles in the *Basic Dictionary* series available from the Canterbury Press:

A Basic Church Dictionary Tony Meakin
Over 10,000 copies sold

A Basic Dictionary of Saints Kathleen Jones

A Basic
Catholic Dictionary

Compiled by
Alan Griffiths

CANTERBURY
PRESS
Norwich

Text © Alan Griffiths 2003
Illustrations © Clive Edwards and Paul Jenkins 2003

First published in 2003 by the Canterbury Press Norwich
(a publishing imprint of Hymns Ancient & Modern Limited,
a registered charity)
St Mary's Works, St Mary's Plain
Norwich, Norfolk, NR3 3BH

www.scm-canterburypress.co.uk

British Library Cataloguing in Publication data

A catalogue record for this book is available
from the British Library

The versions of the Bible used in the preparation of this
book were principally:
The New Revised Standard Version © 1989 by the
National Council of the Churches of Christ in the USA
and *The New Jerusalem Bible* © 1985 by
Darton, Longman and Todd Ltd and Doubleday and Co. Inc.

ISBN 1-85311-525-8

Typeset by Rowland Phototypesetting Ltd,
Bury St Edmunds, Suffolk
Printed and bound in Great Britain by
Bookmarque, Croydon, Surrey

CONTENTS

PREFACE

Many people encounter the Roman Catholic Church through family, friends or business. They sometimes find the jargon we use quite baffling. If people think that the Church is a bit exotic, then this language barrier will do nothing to dispel that. Many Catholics, too, if truth be told, are just as confused.

This book is a modest attempt to help everyone who has ever wondered what the jargon means. It is a *basic* dictionary. It gives the essentials, I hope in relatively simple language. I hope too that it might encourage those who use it to look further and deeper into the wonderful, paradoxical and kaleidoscopic reality that the Church is.

Basic also means that not absolutely everything is in here. That would be *A Comprehensive Catholic Dictionary* – which would just not be ABCD – in any sense! However, I have no doubt left things out by mistake. For this, in advance, I apologise.

The book is in four parts. Part One is the Dictionary, the list of all the words in the book. Words entered in heavy type are defined there and then. Words printed in light type will have page references to the later part(s) where they are defined. These three parts reflect the three traditional roles of the Church: to teach, to make holy and to guide.

The use of an asterisk* in the book means that a term so marked is defined elsewhere and that the definition, or any necessary page references, can be found in the Dictionary section.

I would like to express my thanks to Richard Moth, Vicar General of Southwark Archdiocese, for his help in compiling the Canon Law sections and to Paul Inwood, Diocesan Director of Liturgy in my own Portsmouth Diocese, for his help in compiling the Music section. Numerous others have patiently answered my questions on many other matters. I thank also Christine Smith of the Canterbury Press for presenting me with the idea for the book and for her help and advice throughout.

Alan Griffiths

PART ONE

A DICTIONARY OF
CATHOLIC TERMS

A DICTIONARY OF
CATHOLIC TERMS

Abacus 83

Abba The Aramaic* word for 'Father' used by Jesus* to denote God* and his unique relationship to God, whom he called 'Abba'. Also the term used by early monks* to denote the leader of a monastic community, or a monk who was particularly venerated.

Abbess 122

Abbey 122

Abbot 122

Ablutions 67

Abortion The destruction of the human foetus at any stage after conception. Catholic* teaching holds that human life is sacred, that it begins (at least potentially) at conception and from then on has rights that must be protected.

Abraham The first of the patriarchs*. Abraham (formerly Abram) was the one whose obedience in following God's* call originates the religious tradition today represented by Judaism, Christianity and Islam. His story is told in Genesis* 12–25.

Absolution 67

Absolution, general 73

Abstinence (Latin *abstinentia* – depriving oneself) The act of going without something, e.g. certain foods, for religious reasons. Catholics* abstain from meat on Ash Wednesday* and Good Friday* and perform acts of abstinence on Fridays.

Abutment 83

A cappella 96

Acclamation 96

Acolyte 115

Act of contrition 67

Act of penance see **Penance**

Acts of the Apostles 109

AD (Latin *Anno Domini* – In the year of our Lord*) The dating system that divides world history into before and after the Incarnation* of Christ* was devised in the sixth century by Dionysius Exiguus (died *c*.550CE). The letters AD are used to refer to dates subsequent to the Incarnation, and BC ('Before Christ') to refer to dates before it. Nowadays the use of BCE ('Before Christian Era') and CE ('Christian Era') is preferred as being more historically accurate. The actual date of Christ's birth is unknown, but may have fallen somewhere between 7BCE and 4BCE.

Adam 136

Ad limina (Latin *ad limina Apostolorum* – to the threshold of the apostles*) A pilgrimage* to Rome, to the Apostles Peter* and Paul*. The term is usually used of the obligatory five-yearly visit of bishops* to the Holy See* to report on their dioceses*.

Administrator 144

Adonai (Hebrew for 'majesty') A title of God* in the Old Testament*.

Adoration (Latin *adorare* – to pray towards) Worship* appropriate to God*. The term is also used of a liturgical* act of reverence made towards the Blessed Sacrament*. See **Eucharistic adoration**

Adoro Te 96

Adult baptism 57

Advent, Sundays of 62

Advocate (Latin *ad-vocare* – to call upon) A title of the Holy Spirit* employed in the Gospel of Saint John* and of Christ* himself in the First Letter of John*. It means 'the One who speaks on our behalf before God* the Father. See also **Paraclete**. The term is also used of a clerical* or lay* lawyer appointed by the bishop* to safeguard the rights of someone in a canonical process.

Affinity 151

Affusion 67

Agape (Greek for 'love') (pronounced ag-a-pay) The term used in the New Testament* for self-giving love, also used of the common meal celebrated by early Christians*, sometimes together with the Eucharist*.

Age of reason In Canon Law*, the age at which a person might be presumed able to distinguish between right and wrong. This is normally held to be about seven years of age.

Agnus Dei 96

Aisle 83

Alb 117

Aliturgical day (Greek negative particle *a–*) A day on which the Church* forbids the celebration of Mass*. Good Friday* and Holy Saturday* until the Easter Vigil* are the aliturgical days of the Roman Rite*.

Alleluia 96

All Saints 136

All Souls The title given to the day following All Saints'* Day. It is kept as a commemoration of all the faithful departed*. Mass* is celebrated for the repose of their souls. Some Catholic* communities go in procession to their graveyard that day for prayers*.

Alms (Greek *elemosune* – alms) Relieving poverty or need is one of three traditional ways of obtaining the forgiveness of sins*. As one of the Corporal Works of Mercy* it is particularly recommended during Lent*.

Alpha/omega 130

Altar 67, 83

Altar cloth(s) 67

Altar, high 90

Altar pall 83, 91

Altarpiece 83

Altar rails 83

Altar of repose 83

Ambo 83

Ambulatory 84

A.M.D.G. 130

Amen 97

Amice 117

Amos, Book of 107

Anamnesis 67

Anaphora 68

Anastasis (Greek for 'resurrection') The Resurrection* of Christ*. The term was also used to describe the basilica* erected by Constantine (and much rebuilt since) on the site of the tomb* of Jesus*, known today as the Church of the Holy Sepulchre in Jerusalem.

Anathema (Greek New Testament* meaning 'accursed') From Saint Paul* (Galatians* 1:8–9). Used by the ecumenical councils* of

6

the Church* to condemn heresy*. Use of the term was discontinued at the time of the Second Vatican Council*.

Anchorite/anchoress (Greek *anachorein* – to withdraw) A person who lives in seclusion, leading a life of prayer* and abstinence*.

Ancient of Days A title of God*, used in the Book of Daniel* 7:9 and sometimes translated (as in the New Jerusalem Bible* version) as 'One most venerable'.

Andrew, Saint, Apostle 137

Angel (Greek *angelos* – messenger) Messengers of the invisible God*. In Scripture* angels appear as signs of God's presence, or messengers of God's will. Jesus* spoke of angel guardians, spiritual beings who enjoy the sight of God and will accompany Christ* at his return (Matthew* 22:30, 18:10, 16:27).

Angel (emblem) 130

Angel Gabriel see **Archangel**

Angelus (in Latin, this prayer begins *Angelus Domini nuntiavit Mariae* . . . 'The Angel* of the Lord* brought tidings to Mary* . . .' (cf. Luke* 1:28)). The term given to the prayer* recited three times a day in memory of the Incarnation*.

Angelus bell 84

Anglican (Medieval Latin *anglicus* – English) The term used to describe the Church* of England and the churches associated with it in the worldwide Anglican Communion*.

Anima Christi (opening words of prayer in Latin: *Anima Christi, sanctifica me* . . . 'Soul of Christ*, make me holy . . .') A medieval prayer in honour of the Blessed Sacrament*.

Anna, Saint 137

Anointed One The meaning of the

title 'Christ*' in Greek. It is a translation of Hebrew 'Messiah', also meaning 'God's* anointed', or chosen.

Anointing 68

Anointing of the Sick, Sacrament of 56

Anniversary of dedication see **Dedication of the Church, Solemnity of**

Annulment 150, 151

Annunciation of the Lord, Solemnity of the 66

Antependium 84

Anthem 97

Antiphon 97

Antiphonale Monasticum (Monastic Antiphoner) 97

Antiphonale Romanum (Roman Antiphoner) 97

Antiphoner 97

Apocalypse, Book of the 112

Apocalyptic (Greek *apocalypsis* – revelation) Biblical writing revealing the end of time and the triumph of good over evil. Parts of the Old Testament* Book of Daniel* as well as parts of the New Testament* and the Book of Revelation* are written in this style.

Apologetics (Greek *apologetikos* – defence by argument) The reasoned defence of the Christian* faith* by philosophers or theologians*.

Apostasy (Greek *apostases* – a deserter) The deliberate rejection of Christian faith*.

Apostle 137

Apostles' Creed 49

Apostolate (Greek *apostolos* – someone sent) The title of works done by believers in the name of Christ*. The term is used of the particular works undertaken by religious orders* and communities.

Apostolic (Greek *apostolos* – someone sent) Of or belonging to the apostles*.

Apostolic delegate 143
Apostolic nuncio 144
Apostolic penitentiary 144
Apostolic see 144
Apostolic Signatura 144
Apostolic succession The succession of bishops* from the apostles*. Through ordination* as bishop, the bishop has the office* of teaching, sanctifying and governing the Church* – the mandate given by Christ* to the apostles.

Apparel 118
Appeal tribunal 151
Apse 84
Aramaic The language of Palestine in the time of Christ*. The New Testament* records that Jesus* spoke Aramaic, and it also passed into the liturgical* vocabulary of the early Church*. Examples of this are: *Abba* (Father), Mark* 14:36; *Eloi, eloi, lama sabacthani* (My God, my God, why have you forsaken me?), Mark 15:34; *Ephetha* (Be opened), Mark 7:34; *Maranatha* (Lord! Come!), 1 Corinthians* 16:22; *Talitha kum* (Little girl, I tell you to get up), Mark 5:41.

Arcade 84
Arch- (prefix) 144
Archangel (Greek *archos* – senior, and *angelos* – messenger) In the Old Testament*, angelic beings are mentioned who in Christian* theology* have the title of archangel: Gabriel, Michael*, Raphael (cf. Tobit* 5:4, Luke* 1 and 2, Revelation* 12:7).

Archbishop 144
Archdiocese 144
Architecture, church 81
Architecture, mission 91
Architrave 84
Archpriest 144
Area bishop 144

Arris 84
Ascension of the Lord 65
Ascesis/ticism 122
Ashlar 84
Ash Wednesday see **Lent, season of** 63
Asperges 68
Aspergillum 84
Aspersion (Latin *aspersio* – sprinkling) The rite of sprinkling with holy water*.
Assistant priest 144
Assumption 137
Athanasian Creed 49
Atonement (at-one-ment) An act of reconciliation, of restoring a relationship. In Christian* teaching it is usually used of the reconciliation effected by the death and Resurrection* of Christ*. The Letter to the Hebrews* takes this as its major theme, using the Hebrew festival of *Yom Kippur*, the 'Day of Atonement', as a metaphor for Christ's work of re-establishing the bond between God* and humans. The letter argues that the Day of Atonement is now fulfilled for all time by the death of Jesus*.
Attrition (Latin *attero* – to wear away) Sorrow for sins* arising from the fear of punishment to come.
Auditor 144
Augustinians 122
Aumbry 84
Auxiliary bishop 144
Ave Maria (Latin for 'Hail Mary') The prayer to the Virgin* Mary*, based partly on New Testament* material (in Luke* 1:28, 42) and partly on tradition*. See **Angelus**

Baldacchino 85
Banner 85
Banns 151
Baptism of adults 57
Baptism of blood 68

Baptism of desire 68
Baptism of infants 56
Baptism of the Lord, Feast of the 66
Baptism, Sacrament of 56
Baptismal candle 68
Baptismal font 85
Baptismal garment 68
Baptismal promises 68
Baptismal regeneration see **Regeneration, baptismal**
Baptismal shell 85
Baptismal sponsor 68
Baptismal water 68
Baptistery 85
Baroque (style) 85
Barrel vault 85
Baruch, Book of 106
Basil, Liturgy of Saint One of the three liturgies* for the celebration of the Eucharist* among Orthodox* Christians*. It is thought that the Eucharistic Prayer* of this liturgy was given its present form by Saint Basil the Great (*c*.330–379CE).
Basilica 85
Basilica of Saint Peter see **Peter, Basilica of, Saint (Vatican Basilica)**
Bay 85
BC ('Before Christ') see **AD**
Beam, collar 85
Beam, hammer 85
Beam, tie 85
Beatification 137
Beatitudes (Latin *beatus* – blessed) The sayings of Jesus* in Matthew* 5:3–11, the beginning of the 'Sermon on the Mount' (paralleled in Luke* 6:20–22, the 'Sermon on the Plain'). Each one begins with the word 'Blessed'. They describe the people who are close to God's Kingdom*. The version in Luke adds a set of curses to the list of blessings.
Beelzebub (Hebrew *Baal-zebub*, Greek and Latin *Beelzebul* –

Lord of the Flies) Used in the gospel* to name the prince of devils.
Begotten The word used in the creed* and in the liturgy* ('Begotten, not created') to indicate that Christ* was not created by the Father*, but was of one being with him eternally.
Belfry 85
Belial (Hebrew for 'wickedness') Saint Paul* uses the term to denote Satan*.
Bell, sanctus 78
Bell tower 85
Benedict, Saint, Rule of 122, 127
Benedictines 122
Benediction 68
Benedictus 97
Bible (Greek *biblion* – book) The Scriptures* of the Old* and New Testaments*, as assembled in a single volume. At the time of the production of printed texts in the fifteenth century it became possible to have a whole collection of the Scriptures in one manageable volume. See the section on 'Sacred Scripture', page 101.
Bidding prayer 68
Bier 85
Biretta 118
Bishop 114, 115
Bishop, auxiliary 144
Bishop, coadjutor 145
Bishop, diocesan 146
Bishop, suffragan 149
Bishop, titular Some bishops*, for example auxiliary bishops*, have the title of a diocese* that no longer exists.
Bishopric 144
Bishops, ceremonial of 69, 129
Bishops, college of 146
Bishops' conference see **Episcopal Conference** 146
Blessed 137
Blessed Sacrament 68
Blessed Sacrament, reserva-

9

tion of see **Reservation, Blessed Sacrament** 77

Blessed Virgin Mary 137

Blessing 68

Blessing, nuptial 76

Blood, baptism of 68

Body and Blood of Christ, Solemnity of the 66

Body of Christ The metaphor used by Saint Paul* (1 Corinthians* 12:12–27) to describe the Church* community. The term is also used to describe the Blessed Sacrament*. See also **Mystical body**

Body, resurrection of the see **Resurrection of the body**

Boss 85

Both kinds, Holy Communion 68

Bowing 69

Box, confessional see **Confessional**

Brass 85

Bread: for the Eucharist 69

Bread, breaking of A New Testament* term for the Mass* (cf. Acts* 2:42). See **Eucharist**

Bread, unleavened 80

Breviary 128

Brothers 122

Bugia 85

Bull, papal (Latin *bulla* – seal) A term for important documents issued by the Pope*, sealed with his lead seal.

Burial The practice of placing the bodies of the dead in the earth, where they will decay naturally.

Burse 69

Buttress 85

Buttress, flying 89

Byzantine Rite (Greek city *Byzantium* – modern Istanbul) The liturgy* and other aspects of the life of Christians* who belong to the Orthodox* churches* and some Christians in communion* with the apostolic see*.

Byzantine (style) 85

Calefactory 122

Calendar 62

Calvary (Latin *calvaria* – skull, from Hebrew name *Golgotha* – Place of the Skull) The place of Jesus'* crucifixion*, outside the city of Jerusalem. The site was later included within the walls of the city.

Campanile 85

Candle, baptismal 68

Candle, Easter see **Paschal candle**

Candle, sanctus 78

Candlemas see **Feast of the Presentation of the Lord**

Candles In Christian* prayer* and liturgy* candles are used to symbolise Christ*, the 'Light of the World'. At least two must be lit for Mass*.

Candlesnuffer 86

Canon, honorary 147

Canon (musical) 97

Canon (priest) 144

Canonical 144

Canonical form 144

Canonisation 137

Canon Law 144

Canon of the Mass 69

Canon of Scripture (Greek *kanon* – rule, and Latin *scripturae* – writings) The list of books considered by the Church* since the second century to be authentic Scripture* and containing the inspired witness to Christian faith*.

Canon penitentiary 145

Canons, chapter of see **Chapter of canons**

Canons regular 122

Cantata 97

Canticle 97

Cantillation 97

Cantor 97

Capital 86

Cappa magna 118

Capsa 86

Cardinal 145

Carmelites 122

Carol 97

Carthusians 123

Cartouche 86

Cassock 118

Catafalque 86

Catechism (Greek *katecho* – to instruct, to cause to hear) A manual of Christian* doctrine*. In the Catholic* Church*, the first complete catechism was produced after the Council of Trent* on the model of those written by Martin Luther and other Reformers. The modern *Catechism of the Catholic Church* was produced to reflect the teaching of the Second Vatican Council* and published in 1994.

Catechist (Greek *katecho* – to instruct) A minister* responsible for teaching the faith*, particularly in preparing people to receive the sacraments*.

Catechesis (Greek *katecho* – to instruct) To instruct and nurture the faith* and Christian* life of someone wishing to become a Catholic*.

Catechumen 69

Catechumens, Oil of 76

Catechumenate 69

Cathedra 86

Cathedral 86

Cathedral administrator 144

Catholic (Greek *kat'holon* – throughout the whole [world]) Applied to the Church*, it refers to the universal nature of the Church, in terms of the Church being whole and also complete in every local church*. It also refers to the fullness of Christian* teaching found in the Catholic Church.

Catholic Eastern Churches see **Eastern Churches, Catholic**

Catholic Reformation see **Reformation, Catholic**

Catholics see **Old Catholics, Roman Catholics**

Celebrant 69

Celebration 69

Celibacy 145

Cell 123

Cemetery 86

Cenacle (Latin *coenaculum* – the place for supper) The room, in Jerusalem, where by tradition Jesus* celebrated the Last Supper* with the disciples*.

Censer 69

Censure 145

Ceremonial 69

Ceremonial of Bishops 69

Chair 86

Chalice 69

Chalice veil 69

Chancel 86

Chancellor 145

Chant/chanting 97

Chant, Gregorian 98

Chantry 86

Chantry chapel 86

Chapel 86

Chapel of ease 86

Chapel, Lady 90

Chaplain 145

Chapter 123

Chapter of canons 145

Chapter, general 125

Chapter house 86

Charismata/ic (Greek *charisma/ mata* – gifts/s of grace or of the Spirit) In the sacraments* of baptism* and confirmation*, Christians* receive the gifts necessary to live the life of faith*. With the help of the Holy Spirit*, they should develop and use these gifts in their calling to share with others the 'Kingdom* of God*'. The term is also used of certain specific gifts recorded as having been found in the communities founded by Saint Paul* (see 1 Corinthians* 12:8–11). These include the ability to 'speak in tongues' (to utter sounds in no known language) and to prophesy. In recent years, Catholics* and other Christians have rediscovered this tradition*.

Charity (Greek *charis* – gift, and Latin *caritas* – love) In Old English, charity means active love. In the liturgy*, it describes one of the effects to be hoped for from the Eucharist*. In more modern usage, it refers to acts of charity, or giving to good causes.

Chasuble 118

Cherubim In the Jerusalem Temple, two figures guarding the Ark in the Holy of Holies. Later prophetic tradition* understood them as heavenly beings.

Chevron 86

Children, Directory for Masses with Issued by the Holy See* in 1975, this was a guide to how to celebrate Mass* when the congregation largely consisted of young children below teenage years.

Children, Eucharistic Prayers for Three Eucharistic Prayers* issued in 1975 in association with the Directory for Masses with Children*.

Chi-Rho 130

Choir 86

Choir dress 118

Chrism 69

Christ (Greek *christos* – anointed one, tr. of Hebrew *mashah* – Messiah) The title applied to Jesus* of Nazareth by the earliest Christians*, indicating their faith* in him as the Chosen of God* and the awaited Messiah. The term was used also as a name for Jesus (Galatians* 1:3; Hebrews* 9:11). The followers of Jesus were known as 'Christians'.*

Christ the King, Solemnity of 66

Christ's faithful (Latin *fideles* – believers) The term employed in the Code or Canon Law* to designate the whole membership of the Church*.

Christendom (Old English *Cristendom*) The title, used from the medieval period, for the Christian* world as opposed to the Moslem East.

Christian (Greek *christos* – anointed one or Messiah) The name given to a follower of Christ*. The Acts of the Apostles* (11:26) records that the term was first used at Antioch.

Christian Initiation of Adults, Rite for the see **Rite for the Christian Initiation of Adults**

Christmas 63

Christmas crib 86

Christmas Day 63

Christmas Eve 70

Chronicles, Books of the (1, 2) 103

Chrysostom, Liturgy of Saint John One of the three forms of the Eucharist* in use in the Orthodox Church* and among some Byzantine Rite* Christians* in communion* with the Holy See*.

Church, the (institution) (Greek *kyriakon* – of the Lord) The body of those who believe in Jesus* Christ* as the crucified and Risen One. Catholics* believe that the Church of Christ is the primary sacrament* of his presence in the world and that it subsists in the 'Roman Catholic Church', i.e., those churches in communion* with the Holy See*. The term also describes a particular church, such as the Church of Milan, or the Church in the United States. It is particularly used to denote the building that houses the Christian* community for worship*. It is used as an adjective to describe persons and things associated with the Church: e.g.,

Church worship, etc. See **Body of Christ, Mystical body**

Church (building) The edifice that is used for worship* and fellowship* by Christians*.

Church architecture 81

Church, hall 90

Church, local 147

Church, Orthodox see **Orthodox Church**

Church, parish 148

Church, redundant 86

Churching see **Women, churching**

Churchyard 86

Ciborium 70, 86

Cincture 118

Cistercians 123

Classical orders 86

Clerestory 87

Clergy 145

Clergyman The common title for an ordained* minister*. It is also commonly used as a term to denote the kind of suit and collar worn since the nineteenth century by the ordained. See **Clerical dress**

Cleric (Greek *klerous* – lots cast) Originally, the common title for all the ordained*. Before the liturgical* reforms after the Second Vatican Council*, entry into the clergy* was conferred by a rite of cutting the hair, or tonsure.

Clerical dress The dress required of clergy*. Usually a black or grey suit, black or grey shirt and a white collar, encircling the neck.

Clerical state 145

Cloak 118

Cloister 123

Coadjutor bishop 145

Code 146

Collar beam 85

Collect 70

Collection 70

College (Latin *collegium* – group) A group of people with a defined role in the Church* The term describes the shared ministry* of priests* and bishops*.

College of bishops 146

College of consultors 146

Collegiality The term strictly refers to the exercise of the ministry* of bishops* in communion* with the Pope*. It is more broadly used of any shared authority in the Church*.

Colonnade 87

Colossians, St Paul's Letter to the 110

Colours, liturgical 74

Column 87

Column, engaged 89

Commandments The ten precepts given to Moses (Exodus* 20:1–21; Deuteronomy* 5:2–33). See **Decalogue, Ten Commandments**

Commandments of the Church The Church* imposes six duties on its members: To participate in Mass* on Sundays* and some holy days; to fast* and abstain* on days specified by the Church; to go to the Sacrament of Penance* annually; to receive Holy Communion* during Eastertime*; to contribute to the support of the Church; to observe Church Law governing marriage*. See **Abstinence, Easter duty, Fasting, Holy Days of Obligation**

Common/Ordinary of the Mass 76

Communicant 70

Communion 73, 97

Communion, both kinds 68

Communion, first see **First Communion**

Communion, Holy 73

Communion Rite 58

Communion of saints The spiritual link in grace*, prayer* and good works, that binds the Church* on earth with the saints* and the souls* in Purgatory*.

Competent

Competent 146
Compline 70
Concelebration 70
Concordance (Latin prefix *con* – with, and *cor* – heart, i.e. of one mind/heart) A reference book for Scripture*, giving references for all the places where a particular word is found. The most famous concordance is that of Alexander Cruden, first published in 1737, but with many later editions.
Conference of bishops see **Episcopal conference**
Confession 71
Confession, sacramental 59
Confessional 87
Confessor (Latin *confiteor* – I confess) A spiritual guide, usually but not necessarily a bishop* or priest*, to whom Catholics* may go to confess their sins* and receive support in their life as believers.
Confessor 137
Confirmation, Sacrament of 57
Congregation 146
Congregations, missionary 125
Congress, eucharistic see **Eucharistic congress**
Conopaeum 87
Consanguinity 151
Consecration 71
Consecration cross 87
Consent 151
Consultors, college of 146
Consummated 151
Contemplation (Latin prefix *con* – with, and *templum* – place of seeing) See **Prayer**
Contrition (Latin prefix *con* – with, and *terere* – to wear away) True sorrow for sin* and determination to cease from sin.
Convent 123
Conventual 124
Conversion (Latin prefix *con* – with, and *vertere* – to turn) The process whereby a person becomes a

Christian* believer, and a member of the Church* through baptism* and confirmation*.
Cope 118
Corbel 87
Corinthian order 88
Corinthians, Saint Paul's Letters to the (1, 2) 109
Cornice 88
Corona 88
Coronation A devotional act usually to images of the Blessed Virgin Mary*, where a small crown is placed on the head of the image, and also upon the head of Christ*, if a representation of Christ is part of the image.
Corporal 71
Corporal works of mercy (Latin *corporalis* – bodily) The works mentioned in the Parable of the Sheep and Goats in Matthew* 25:31–46: feeding the hungry, giving drink to the thirsty, welcoming the stranger, clothing the naked, visiting the sick, helping those in prison. In addition, burying the dead makes up the number seven.
Corpus Christi 66
Cosmatesque 88
Cotta 118
Council, ecumenical (Greek *oikumene*, the whole world) The term denoting the highest assembly of the bishops* of the Catholic Church*, called by the Pope* to discuss and legislate theological and disciplinary matters.
Council, episcopal 146
Council, parish pastoral see **Parish council**
Council of priests 146
Counter Reformation see **Reformation, Catholic**
Course, string 94
Covenant In Scripture*, the relationship between God* and God's people. Noah and Abraham* and

14

most significantly Moses* formed covenants. The Covenant of Moses was expressed in the Law, or Torah*. See also **Testament**

Covenant (biblical) (Latin prefix *con* – with, and *venire* – to come) The relationship between God* and God's chosen people in Scripture*, in which God protects and favours his people in return for their allegiance. A covenant was made with Noah after the Flood, when God promised that no more floods would destroy the earth (Genesis* 9:8); another covenant was made with Abraham, God promising him the land of Caanan and numerous offspring (Genesis 15:18); the covenant made after the escape from Egypt was the most important, reflecting Israel's promise of obedience to the Torah and God's promise to protect and prosper them (Exodus* 19, 20). The Prophets* developed the idea of covenant, placing importance on its ethical significance (see, e.g., Jeremiah* 31:31). The New Testament* sees a new covenant being made through the death and Resurrection* of Jesus* (e.g., Matthew* 26:28), but this time with Gentiles* as well as Jews, whose observance was not that of rules, but that of a change of heart and lifestyle to follow the gospel*.

Covenant, local ecumenical (Greek *oecumene* – the whole world) An agreement between Christian* communities in a given area to work together, with the intention of working for Christian unity*.

Creator (Latin *creator* – maker) A title of God*, who made all things. More specifically, the title is used of the Holy Spirit* in the

liturgy*, as in the hymn *Veni Creator Spiritus* ('Come, Creator Spirit').

Credence 88

Credo 49

Creed 71

Creed, Apostles' 49

Creed, Athanasian 49

Creed, Nicene 49

Cremation (Latin *cremare* – to reduce to ashes) Disposal of a corpse by fire. The Catholic* Church* used not to favour cremation, because in some countries it was employed deliberately as an anti-Catholic practice.

Crib, Christmas see **Christmas crib**

Crocket 88

Crosier 118

Cross 71, 88, 130

Cross, consecration 87

Cross keys 131

Cross, Jerusalem 90

Cross, Latin 90

Cross, pectoral 120

Cross, processional 92

Cross, sign of the Tracing the cross* on the forehead, chest, left and right shoulder. Catholics* commonly use this to begin any act of prayer* or worship*.

Cross, Stations of the 79

Cross, Way of the 80

Crossing 88

Crown 131

Crown of thorns 131

Crucifix 88

Crucifixion (Latin *cruci-fixus* – fixed to a cross) The method used to execute Jesus*. The Romans employed crucifixion as a penalty for slaves or those who were not Roman citizens. The subject was nailed or lashed on to two wooden beams set crosswise, in such a way as to cause a slow death* by suffocation. Crucifixion was abolished by the Emperor Constantine in the fourth century CE. See also **Cross**

Cruciform 88

Cruets 71

Crypt 88

Cult 71

Curate 146

Cure (of souls) 146

Curia 146

Curia, Roman 148

Cursillo Movement 124

Curtilage 88

Cusp 88

Czestochowa, Marian Shrine 137

Daily Prayer see **Liturgy of the Hours** and **Divine Office**

Dalmatic 118

Dame 124

Daniel, Book of 106

Day, Lady The old title for the feast* of the Annunciation of Christ* to Mary* on 25 March. See **Annunciation of the Lord**

Day, Lord's see **Lord's Day**

Days, ember and rogation see **Ember days** and **Rogations**

Deacon 115

Dean 146

Deanery 146

Deanery pastoral council 146

Death, christian The Church* sees death as connected to Adam's* sin* (Romans* 5:12), but not as the end of life, since the faith* of the Church in the Resurrection* of Jesus* opens up the hope* of eternal life. The Funeral Liturgy* of the Church is based on faith in the Risen Christ*

Decalogue (Greek *deka* – ten, and *logos* – word) Another term for the Ten Commandments*.

Decorated 88

Decree 146

Decree (of nullity) see **Nullity**

Dedication of a church 71

Defect 151

Defender of the bond 151

Degrees of affinity 151

Delegate, apostolic see **Apostolic delegate**

Demythologisation The reinterpretation of Scripture* to explain elements that contemporary readers would regard as unscientific and therefore untrue or mythical. Demythologisation began in the nineteenth century among Scripture scholars and has been highly influential. It is claimed that the process allows a clearer picture of biblical events and personalities to emerge. However, demythologisation itself is subject to criticism, in that it is said to take insufficient account of the literary *genres* found in Scripture, such as myth, which, while not factual, is still theologically significant.

Denomination (Latin *denominare* – to give a name) The term used to describe different Church* groups within the Christian* tradition*, e.g., Anglican,* Catholic*, Methodist etc.

Deposit of faith The body of revelation* and tradition* which forms the teaching of the Church*.

Desire, baptism of 68

Deus in adjutorium (Latin for 'O God, come to my aid') The first verse of Psalm* 70 and from the time of the Rule of Saint Benedict*, the usual way of beginning the celebration of the Hours. See **Liturgy of the Hours**

Deuteronomy, Book of 102

Devil (Greek *diabolos* – accuser) In Scripture*, the one who tests Jesus* in the desert (Matthew* 4:5), the persuader of evil, sometimes also termed 'Satan'*.

Devotions 71

Diaconate 115

Diaper 88

Diocesan bishop 146

Diocese 146

Diocesan exorcist see **Exorcist, diocesan**

Diocesan pastoral council 146

Diocesan synod 146

Direction, spiritual The practice of talking about one's Christian* beliefs and life with someone who is helping to deepen and focus or guide them.

Directory, Documents of Bishops' Conference In accordance with their teaching and governing role in the Church*, bishops* from time to time issue directories, collections of rules on particular subjects. These have the force of law in the territory of the bishops' conference* concerned.

Directory, for Masses with children see **Children, Directory for Masses with**

Disciple 137

Dish, lavabo 74

Dismissal 71

Disparity of worship 151

Dispensation (Latin *dispensatio* – a setting aside) The relaxing of Church* Law in particular cases for good reasons.

Dispensation 151

Divine Office 71

Divine revelation see **Revelation, divine**

Divorce, Church and civil 151

Doctrinal (Latin *docere* – to teach) Of or pertaining to doctrine*.

Doctrine (Latin *docere* – to teach) The collection of teaching of a particular denomination* or Church*.

Dogma (Greek *dogma* – that which seems the case) In the Catholic* Church*, a truth revealed by God* and articulated as an infallible teaching by the Church.

Dogmatic theology (Greek *dogma*

– that which seems to be the case) The tradition* of study and exposition of basic Christian* teachings on creation, redemption* and salvation*.

D.O.M. 131

Dom 124

Dome 88

Dominical (Latin *dominus* – Lord, Master) Of, or belonging to, Christ* (the Lord*).

Dominicans 124

Doric order 88

Dormer window 88

Dorsal 88

Dove 131

Doxology 97

Dress, choir see **Choir dress**

Dress, clerical see **Clerical dress**

Eagle 131

Early English 88

Ease, chapel of 86

Easter candle see **Paschal candle**

Easter duty The commandment of the Church* that obliges Catholics* to receive Communion* annually, preferably during the Easter Season*.

Easter mystery see **Paschal mystery**

Easter Sunday and Eastertime 64, 65

Easter Vigil 65

Easter Week The week following Easter Sunday*.

Eastern Churches, Catholic Churches* of the Byzantine Rite* and other Eastern rites that are in communion* with the Holy See*. They have their own liturgy*, Canon Law* and other customs.

Eastern Churches, Separated Those Byzantine Rite* and other Eastern churches* not in communion* with the Holy See*. The Catholic* Church* respects them as churches possessing authentic ministry* and sacraments*.

Ecclesiastes 104

Ecclesiastical (Greek *ekklesia* – Church) Of or pertaining to the Church*.

Ecclesiastical exemption 88

Ecclesiasticus, Book of 105

Ecclesiology That part of theology* which reflects on the mystery* of the Church*. See also page 89.

Ecumenical council 50–1

Ecumenical Movement (Greek *oecumene* – the whole world) The movement begun in the twentieth century to unite the Christian* denominations*. More recently, this has been developed into a desire to bring separate denominations closer together, by recognising each other's ministries* and practices. The Second Vatican Council* recognised the legitimacy of this movement.

Ecumenism see **Ecumenical Movement**

Effigy 89

Elect 71

Election, Rite of 77

Elements 71

Elevation (architectural) 89

Elevation (eucharistic) 71

Elohim (Hebrew – 'the gods') used in the Old Testament* to describe the God* of Israel. The Pentateuch* was composed of material from several sources, one of which was named 'elohistic' because in it God is named as 'Elohim'.

Ember days (Old English *ymbryne* – period) Ember days occurred four times a year, on a Wednesday, Friday and Saturday in the week after the First Sunday* of Lent*, the week after the Feast* of Pentecost* and the week after the seventeenth Sunday after Pentecost (usually in September) and the week after the Third Sunday of Advent*. They had special texts for the Mass*, were fasting days, and ordinations* often took place on them. Ember days were abolished in the reform of the liturgy* in 1969, and bishops' conferences* were invited to fix times for special public prayer*. See also **Family fast days**

Emblems of the evangelists 131

Emeritus (Latin for 'one who has earned') A retired person who retains the title of their office*.

Emmanuel (Hebrew for 'with us is God') A title for one whom God* will send in Isaiah* 7:14 and 8:8. The New Testament* uses it as a title of Christ* (Matthew* 1:23).

Empty tomb see **Easter**

Encaustic tile 89

Enclosure 124

Encyclical A letter from the Pope* to all the churches* on a serious matter of universal concern. Encyclical letters are the highest form of teaching apart from infallible dogmatic* statements. See **Letter, (papal) encyclical**

Engaged column 89

Enquiry 71

Entablature 89

Ephesians, Saint Paul's Letter to the 110

Epiclesis 72

Epiphany 63

Episcopal (Greek *episcopos* – overseer) Of or belonging to a bishop*.

Episcopal conference 146

Episcopal council 146

Episcopal vicar 146

Episcopate 146

Epistle 72

Epistle side 89

Eschatology (Greek *eschata* – last things, and *logos* – discourse) A theological term for the study of God's* final destiny for creation. In the Old Testament* this theology* is closely bound up with the prophets'* view of the people's infidelity, God's judgement*, the identity and role of the Messiah* and concepts such as the 'Day of the Lord' (cf. Amos* 5:18–20). Jesus* himself seems to have spoken of a day when God would judge the world amid scenes of universal overthrow (Luke* 17:22–36). Such themes are the main topic of the Apocalypse*.

Esther, Book of 103

Eternal (Latin *aeternus* – outside of time) Something that exists uninfluenced by time and change. Strictly speaking, it differs from 'everlasting' in that the former is a time-related concept, while 'eternal' is outside time.

Eucharist, Liturgy of the 75

Eucharist, Sacrament of 72

Eucharistic adoration 72

Eucharistic congress National or international gatherings to reflect on the Eucharist*. The first such conference was held in France in 1931.

Eucharistic exposition see **Exposition, eucharistic**

Eucharistic fast 72

Eucharistic minister see **Minister, extraordinary of communion**

Eucharistic Prayer 72

Eucharistic Prayers of Reconciliation see **Reconciliation, Eucharistic Prayers of**

Evangelical (Greek *evangelion* – good news, gospel) Of or pertaining to the gospel*. The term is used also of Christians* who claim to take the Gospels literally as a basis for a personal knowledge of Jesus*.

Evangelisation (Greek *evangelion* – good news, gospel) The bringing of the Christian* gospel* to everyone, both by teaching and example.

Evangelist 137

Evangelists, emblems of the 131

Eve see **Adam**

Evening Prayer 72

Ewer 72

Examination of conscience The process of remembering faults and sins, used as a preparation for the Sacrament of Penance* and at other times.

Excommunication (Latin *excommunicare* – to cut off) The act of formally excluding a Catholic* from the sacraments* for some serious reason. It is little used nowadays.

Exedra 89

Exemption, ecclesiastical see **Ecclesiastical exemption**

Exercises, Spiritual see **Retreat**

Exodus, Book of 102

Exorcism (Greek *ex-orkizein* – to expel by oath or curse) The ritual*, authorised by the Church*, to expel demons from those who are possessed. Exorcism is not used in the Catholic* Church unless it is certain that the problem is not of psychological origin.

Exorcist, diocesan Each bishop* appoints a priest* whose job is to discern the causes of apparent possession and perform exorcism* in appropriate cases.

Expiation (Latin *expiare* – to make amends for) To make amends for an offence or sin*. Christian* teaching is that Christ* himself made the perfect act of expiation by his death and Resurrection*.

Exposition (eucharistic) 72

Exsultet 97

Extraordinary minister of Communion 115

Ezekiel, Book of 106

Ezra, Book of 103

Faculty 146

Faith (Latin *fides* – faith) Two meanings are implicit in this term:

either the *act of faith*, an act of the will by which the believer responds to God's* initiative and truth, and exercises a relationship of trust in and dependence on the God revealed in Jesus* Christ*, or intellectual assent to the *content of faith* which is the body of those things God has revealed* through the apostles* and the Church*. Faith is God-given, one of the three 'theological' (God-given) virtues*.

Faith, Catholic see **Faith**

Faith, deposit of see **Deposit of faith**

Faith, promoter of the see **Promoter of the faith**

Faithful, Christ's see **Christ's faithful**

Faithful departed (Latin *fideles* – believers) Those who have died in the Christian faith*.

Faldstool 89

Fall 89

Fall, the The term used to denote the belief that the human race has 'fallen out' of harmony with its Creator. The Fall is told symbolically in Genesis* 3 as a story of the eating of fruit from a tree forbidden to Adam* and Eve, and echoed in the other narratives of Genesis 1–12: Cain and Abel, Noah and the Flood, the Tower of Babel. See **Original Sin**

Fan vault 89

Fast 72

Father 147

Father, God the Jesus* spoke of God* as his 'Abba' (Aramaic for 'Papa') and taught the disciples to pray in that same mode. See **Abba, Our Father**

Fathers of the Church Orthodox* writers and preachers of the early centuries of the Church* whose work laid the foundations of belief. They are usually referred to as either the Greek or Latin Fathers, depending on the language they wrote in.

Fatima 138

Féast 72

Feasts, moveable see **Moveable feasts**

Feet, washing of In the Mass* of Maundy or Holy Thursday*, the priest* washes the feet of his parishioners* as Jesus* did at the Last Supper* (John* 13:1–15). There is debate over whether twelve men should have their feet washed (making the rite a sort of pageant of Christ* at the Last Supper) or whether more people, including women, should take part, making it more of a symbol of the Church* serving the needy.

Fellowship The communion* or 'being together' of believers in the Church*.

Feretory 89

Feria 72

Ferial 72

Filioque (Latin for 'and from the Son') The Latin Nicene Creed* has this word attached to the reference to the Holy Spirit*. The original text read: '. . . who proceeds from the Father' but the Spanish Council of Toledo (589CE) added 'and from the Son (*filioque*)'. The Orthodox Church* does not use the term, saying that there is only one fount of divinity, the Father*. The *Filioque* is increasingly omitted in recitation of the Creed in many churches*.

Fillet 89

Final commendation and farewell 72

Finial 89

Fire, new 76

First Communion A child will normally receive Holy Communion* for the first time at about age seven or eight, after due preparation.

First Fridays An act of piety* to the Sacred Heart*, in which a person will receive Communion* on the first Friday of nine consecutive months, in hope of the gift of repentance* at the time of death*.

First instance, Court of 147

Fish 131

Flagon 72

Fleche 89

Flute/d 89

Flying buttress 89

Focolare Movement 124

Font 89

Footpace 89

Forgiveness see **Remission**

Form, canonical 151

Form of marriage 151

Form, sacramental 72

Forty Hours Devotion 72

Fraction 73

Franciscans 124

Friar 125

Friars Minor 125

Friary 125

Fridays, First see **First Fridays**

Friday, Good 65

Frieze 89

Frontal 89

Fundamentalism (Latin *fundamentum* – foundation) The doctrine* that every word of the Scriptures* is literally true. The Catholic* Church* does not hold this doctrine.

Funeral pall 89

Funeral rite 61

Galatians, Saint Paul's Letter to the 110

Galilee The area to the north of Judaea, and the place of origin of Jesus*. It had a mixed population, and was turbulent. The term is also used in church* architecture to describe a large western porch* or narthex*.

Gallery 89

Gargoyle 89

Garment, baptismal 68

Gaudete Sunday (Latin *gaudete* – rejoice!) The Third Sunday of Advent*, so called after the opening words of the Introit* for the Mass* of that day, from Philippians* 4:4. Rose vestments* may be worn instead of purple.

Gradine 90

Gehenna The valley of Hinnom, to the south of Jerusalem, known originally as a place of human sacrifice*. It was used as an image of Hell*.

General absolution 73

General chapter 125

Genesis, Book of 101

Gentile (Latin *gentilis* – foreigner) The term used by Jews to describe a non-Jew.

Genuflection 73

Ghost, Holy see **Holy Spirit**

Girdle 118

Glass, stained/coloured 94

Gloria in Excelsis 97

Gloria Patri 97

Glory 89

Glory be 97

Glory to God in the highest 98

God The being than whom no greater being can be named. The Church* teaches that God is spirit, that God is Creator and Sustainer of everything, self-sufficient and beyond anything we can conceive, speak or imagine. However, by revelation*, God has revealed the Godhead* as Father*, Son* and Spirit*, the Trinity*.

Godhead The nature of God*.

Godparent see **Sponsor**

Good Friday 65

Gospel 73

Gospel side 89

Gospels, Synoptic 108

Gothic 89

Gothic Revival 90

Grace (Latin *gratia* – translating Greek *charis* – gift) The love and kindness of God*, freely given, particularly in the life, death* and Resurrection* of Christ* and the gift of the Holy Spirit*. Medieval theology* identified three types of grace: 'uncreated', referring to God's presence; 'sanctifying', a sharing in the life of God; and 'actual', the ongoing help of God in the life of believers.

Grace before/after meals Prayers* said before eating, usually in the form of a thanksgiving.

Gradual 73

Graduale Romanum (Roman Gradual) 98

Graduale Simplex (Simple Gradual) 98

Grail, the 125

Grave sin see **Mortal sin**

Gregorian chant 98

Gridiron 132

Grille 90

Groin 90

Guadaloupe 138

Habakkuk, Book of 107

Habit 125

Hades (Greek *aides* – the place of the dead) The Greek term for Hebrew *Sheol*.

Haggai, Book of 107

Hail Mary The prayer* in honour of Our Lady*, composed of verses from the Gospel* of Luke* (1, 28, 42) and traditional material.

Hall church 90

Hallelujah see **Alleluia**

Halo 132

Hammer beam 85

Hands, imposition of 73

Hanging pyx 90

Harvest Thanksgiving The Sunday* between 22 and 28 September is kept as a day of prayer* and thanksgiving for the harvest and the fruits of human work.

Hassock 90

Healing There is no formal 'healing ministry'* in the Catholic* Church*. However, the Rite of Anointing of the Sick* speaks of the Sacrament* of anointing as a source of healing and salvation*, if God* wills.

Hearse 90

Heart (pierced) 132

Heaven The Hebrew tradition*, in common with other religions, conceived of God* as a god of the heavens (though God's transcendence* places God 'above' the heavens, cf. Psalm* 113:4), and the idea passed into Christianity*. Christ's 'Ascension'* into heaven appears in the Gospel of Luke* and the Acts of the Apostles* as a way of alluding to his glory and title of '*Kyrios*' or Lord. Heaven is used as a metaphor denoting the presence of God; the term is used metaphorically to describe the place to which believers hope* to go eventually after death*.

Hebrews, Letter to the 111

Hell Related probably to words denoting holes and pits, the term describes the total and irrevocable absence of God*, to which people may come who have truly, absolutely and consistently rejected God's love and justice in favour of their own self-centredness. Theologians* take differing views on the 'existence' of Hell and whether anyone is there.

Heresy (Greek *hairesis* – choice, sect) Denial of an orthodox* truth of the faith* of the Church*.

Hermit (Greek *eremos* – desert) One who withdraws from the world (originally to the desert) to serve God* in solitude.

Hermitage (Greek *eremos* – desert) The dwelling of a hermit*.

Hierarchy (Greek *hiereus* – priest, and *archos* – senior) The name given to the ordained* ministry* of the Church*, particularly the Pope* and bishops*.

High altar 90

High Mass 73

Historic Churches Committee In England and Wales, the committee set up under the ecclesiastical exemption* to assist the bishop* in granting a faculty* for works to take place on a Church building protected by legislation.

Holy Communion 73

Holy days of obligation Those days in the year when Catholics* must attend Mass*. Canon Law* recognises all Sundays*, Christmas Day*, Epiphany*, Ascension Day, Corpus Christi*, the Mother of God*, the Immaculate Conception*, the Assumption*, Saints Peter* and Paul* and All Saints*.

Holy Ghost 'Ghost' is Old English for 'Spirit'. See **Holy Spirit**

Holy Holy Holy 98

Holy order 56, 59, 73

Holy Saturday 65

Holy See (Latin *sedes* – seat) A term for the bishopric* of Rome, the seat of the Pope*. See also **Apostolic see**

Holy Spirit (Latin *spiritus* – spirit, related to 'breath') The Third Person of the Trinity*. The Holy Spirit is distinct from the Father* and the Son*, but equal to them. The Holy Spirit operates in the sacraments*, in the teaching of the Church* and in the life of believers.

Holy table 73

Holy A term describing God* as utterly 'other' and transcendent. It is also used as an adjective for many things in the Church*.

Holy Thursday 65

Holy Trinity, Solemnity of the 66

Holy water 73

Holy Week 64

Homily 73

Homoousion (Greek for 'the same as') 'Of one substance, equal in being', the term describing the status of the Son* in relation to the Father*. The term was used at the Council* of Nicaea.

Honorary canon 147

Hood 118

Hope (theological virtue) The God-given capacity to look beyond this life to the Resurrection*.

Hosanna 73

Hosea, Book of 106

Host 73

Hosts, Lord God of see **Sabaoth**

Hours, Liturgy of the 60

Humeral veil 118

Hymn 98

I.C.E.L. (International Commission for English in the Liturgy) The body set up after the Second Vatican Council* in 1965 to translate Latin liturgical* books for the English-speaking world. I.C.E.L. is a commission of bishops* who, with their experts and consultors, produce translations for conferences of bishops to approve and publish, subject to further approval from the Holy See*.

Icon (ikon) 90

Iconostasis 90

Icthys see **Fish**

Ignatius of Loyola, Saint see **Jesuits** 125

I.H.S. 132

Image (Latin *imago*) A picture or statue of Christ* or a saint*, placed in a church* for veneration.

Image of God (Latin *imago* [*Dei*] – image [of God]) The Genesis creation myth (Genesis* 1:26) speaks of humankind being created in the image or likeness of

God*. Later theology* locates the divine likeness in human free will, reason, moral nature and the desire for God.

Immaculate Conception 138

Immanence (Latin *in-manere* – to dwell within) The belief that God*, though transcendent, is present to his creation.

Immersion 73

Impeded 147

Impediment 152

Imposition of hands 73

Impost 90

Imprimatur Official approval, usually given by a bishop*, that a book or text of theology*, scriptural or catechetical material is in agreement with the teaching of the Church*.

Incardination (Latin *in* – in, and *cardo* – hinge) The act whereby a cleric* is made part of a diocese* or religious order*.

Incarnate (Latin *incarnatus* – being made in flesh or body) The creeds* affirm that the eternal Son and Word of God (cf. John 1:1, 14) assumed a human body from his human Mother as Jesus of Nazareth.

Incarnation (Latin *caro* – flesh, so *incarnatio* – enfleshment) The term denoting the coming of the eternal Son* of God* into this universe in human form, by the agency of the Holy Spirit* and birth from the Blessed Virgin Mary*.

Incense 74

Indulgences (Latin *indulgentia* – remission) The remission of any punishment due for sin*, where guilt is already forgiven. This may be gained by the performance of certain religious actions, which the Church* names as 'indulgences.' Certain prayers* at certain times and in certain places

(such as pilgrimage* shrines*) are 'indulgences'.

Infallibility The doctrine* that in fundamental matters of faith* and morals, the teaching of the Church* is preserved by the Holy Spirit* from the possibility of error. This gift resides in the person of the Pope* when, acting as successor of Peter*, and teacher of the universal Church, he proclaims a doctrine of faith and morals. Infallibility also resides in the college of bishops* when they exercise this teaching office in union with the Pope.

Infant baptism 56

Infant of Prague see **Prague, Infant of**

In petto see **Petto, in**

Inquisition A Church* court that tried charges of heresy*. It was founded in 1232. The more notorious Spanish Inquisition of the fifteenth century was independent of the Roman Inquisition and often failed to act with due consideration towards the accused, frequently employing torture and death*, whereas the original purpose of the inquisition was to encourage conversion* of heretics.

I.N.R.I. 132

Inspiration, biblical The doctrine* that the Scriptures* transmit to us the true word* of God*, by the Holy Spirit*, that God is their 'author' and that the Church* transmits them to us.

Installation 147

Institute, secular see **Secular institute**

Institution, words of 74

Instruments of the Passion 132

Intercession 74

Interdict 147

Interment The burial* of a body in the earth.

Interregnum 147
Intinction 74
Intone 98
Introit 98
Invocation (Latin *invocare* – to call upon) The Holy Spirit* is invoked in the Eucharistic Prayer* to make the bread* and wine* the body and blood of Christ*. Invocation is also made to ask the prayers* of the saints*.
Ionic order 90
Isaiah, Book of 105

James, Letter of 111
James, Liturgy of Saint One of the three forms of the eucharistic liturgy* in use among the Orthodox* churches*.
Jansenism A heresy* of the seventeenth century which held that after the Fall*, human nature was irrecoverably corrupt and only those chosen by God* could be saved. It taught a strict morality, and though condemned by Pope* Innocent X in 1653, it continued to exercise great influence in parts of the Church*, particularly in France and Ireland.
Jehovah An anglicised and vocalised version of the four consonants forming the name of God* given to Moses (cf. Exodus* 3:14) in the Old Testament*. In Hebrew worship* and Christian* liturgy* this name of God is not pronounced. The term 'Lord'* is always substituted.
Jeremiah, Book of 106
Jerusalem cross 90
Jesse window 90
Jesuits 125
Jesus The Greek/Latin version of the Hebrew name 'Joshua' or 'God saves' (Matthew* 1:21), given by Mary* and Joseph to the infant Jesus. See also **Christ**
Jesus Prayer 74

Joachim, Saint 138
Job, Book of 104
Joel, Book of 106
John the Baptist 138
John, Gospel of Saint 108
John, Letters of (1, 2, 3) 112
John, Saint 138
Jonah, Book of 107
Joshua, Book of 102
Jude, Letter of 112
Judgement Catholic* teaching is that there are two judgements. Each person is judged immediately after death*. This is known as the Particular Judgement, in contrast to the General Judgement which will take place at the end of time. The Apostles' Creed* and Nicene Creed* only speak of the General Judgement. See Matthew* 25:31–46 and 2 Thessalonians* 2:3–10. The sense of this is that human beings are free individuals who have to answer for their actions.
Judges, Book of 102
Judicial vicar 147
Judith, Book of 103
Justification (Latin *justum facere* – to make just) Since human beings are born in 'Original Sin'* or alienation from God*, God in Christ* reconciles them, forgives sin* and offers grace* to make them holy*, restoring the intimacy with God for which they were created.

Kerygma (Greek for 'proclamation') The preaching of the good news of salvation*. See **Gospel**
Keys, power of An expression denoting the role of the priest* to absolve in the Sacrament of Penance*.
Keys, Saint Peter's see **Cross Keys**
Kinds, Holy Communion, both Communion* given both from the consecrated bread* and the cup.

25

This became the usual practice in English-speaking countries in 1987, but had previously been allowed on selected occasions by the Vatican* Council.

Kingdom of God/Heaven Better translated as 'the rule of God' revealed in the person, teaching and actions of Jesus* Christ* (see for example Matthew* 13:24–33). The Church* is called by Christ to proclaim the rule of God*, and sees itself as the beginnings of that rule. In the liturgy*, the feast* of Christ the King* is celebrated each year on the Sunday* before Advent*.

King post 90

Kings, Books of (1, 2) 103

Kiss of peace see **Sign of peace**

Kneeling (Saxon *cneow* – knee) A liturgical* posture of repentance* and adoration*.

Knights of the Holy Sepulchre Founded in 1103 as a religious* order* dedicated to the protection of the Latin Diocese* of Jerusalem, the order nowadays exists to support the work of the Catholic* Church* in the Holy Land.

Knights of Malta The Military Hospitaller Order* of Saint John of Jerusalem, Rhodes and Malta, founded in the twelfth century as one of the religious orders taking their inspiration partly from monks* and partly from Crusaders.

Knights of Saint Columba An organisation of Catholic* men, which supports the Church* in practical matters and cares for its own members, and the widows and dependants of deceased members.

Kyrie eleison 98

Kyrios (Greek for 'Lord') This title is used of God* in the Greek Old Testament*. It is used of Christ* by Saint Paul* and elsewhere in the New Testament* to demonstrate faith* in Christ's divine Sonship, glory and reign.

Lady chapel 90

Lady Day see **Day, Lady**

Lady, Our 136

Laetare Sunday (Latin *laetare* – rejoice!) A name given to the Fourth Sunday* of Lent*, taken from the opening of the Introit* for that day from Isaiah* 66:10. Rose vestments* may be worn instead of purple.

Laicisation (Greek *laos* – the people) In Canon Law*, the return of an ordained* person to the legal status of a lay* person.

Laity (Greek *laos* – the people) All the people of the Church*. The term is now used to denote the members of the Church who are neither ordained* nor in a religious* order*.

Lamb 132

Lamb, paschal 133

Lamentations, Book of 106

Lamp 90

Lancet window 90

Lantern 90

Lapsed A term formerly in use to describe Catholics* who do not attend Mass*.

La Salette 138

Last rites The term formerly given to the Sacrament of Anointing*, which became reserved to the dying in the Middle Ages. The rite of Viaticum* is the proper ritual for those near death*.

Last Supper 74

Lateran The Cathedral of the Pope is the Basilica* of Saint John. It is in the Lateran, built by the Emperor Constantine and dedicated to Christ* the Saviour*. It is adjacent to the palace owned formerly by the Laterani family.

The palace was given by Constantine to Pope Sylvester, and was the residence of the Pope* until the fifteenth century.

Latin cross 90

Lauds 74

Lavabo 74

Lavabo dish 74

Lavabo towel 74

Law see **Canon Law**

Lay 115

Lay ministries 115

Laying on of hands see **Imposition of hands**

Lectern 90

Lectionary 128

Lectio divina (Latin for 'holy reading') The practice of slow, meditative reading of Scripture*.

Lector 115

Legion of Mary A lay* association promoting devotion* to Our Lady* and assisting in the work of evangelisation*.

Lent, Season of 63

Lent, Sundays of 63

Lenten abstinence (Latin *abstinere* – to abstain) To go without some food, drink or other pleasure during Lent*.

Lenten scrutinies see **Scrutinies**

Lenten veil 74

Letter (papal), encyclical A papal 'circular' letter, addressed to all Christians* and sometimes to all human beings. A highly authoritative form of Church* teaching. See **Encyclical**

Letter, pastoral (Latin *pastor* – shepherd) The letter written by the diocesan bishop* to mark events or seasons* or to give teaching, which must be read in churches*.

Letters of Saint Paul 109

Leviticus, Book of 102

Liber Cantualis 98

Liber Usualis 98

Lierne vaulting 91

Light In Scripture* and Christian* tradition*, light is associated with God* as an attribute or image of the divine being. Later Christian tradition drew on this to express in buildings the image of divine light. The Gothic* style, with its technology allowing large areas of glass, was a response to this mystical tradition. Painters of the Baroque* period used light to show the divine presence and, more recently, architects have tried to maximise natural light in churches*.

Light (windows) 91

Lilies 132

Lintel 91

Lion 133

Litany 74

Litany of the Saints 74

Liturgical 74

Liturgical colours 74

Liturgical Movement The movement in the nineteenth- and twentieth-century Catholic Church* to recognise the importance of the liturgy* as the prayer of Christ* the Head in the Church, his body, by the power of the Holy Spirit*; to restore participation in the liturgy and to reform the liturgy. Pope* Pius XII recognised the importance of the movement in 1947 confirming its main themes in his encyclical letter 'Mediator Dei'. The Second Vatican Council* ordered this wholesale reform.

Liturgy 75

Liturgy of the Eucharist 75

Liturgy of the Hours 75

Liturgy of Saint Basil see **Basil, Liturgy of Saint**

Liturgy of Saint James see **James, Liturgy of Saint**

Liturgy of Saint John Chrysostom see **Chrysostom, Liturgy of Saint John**

Liturgy of the Word 75

Local church 147

Local ecumenical covenant see **Covenant, local ecumenical**

Local ordinary 147

Loft, rood 93

Logos (Greek for 'the Word'*) A title of Christ*, emphasising his pre-existence from the beginning, found particularly in the Gospel of John* (e.g., John 1:1–18). Greek philosophy used the term to describe the 'why' of all existence. The *logos* was the universal 'reason' for everything. In the Old Testament* the 'Word' of God* was God's creative action, as well as his way of communicating with creation. In Wisdom Literature*, the Word is seen as almost an incarnation* of God (see Wisdom* 1:6, 7; 7:22–26). The Gospel of John identifies this 'Word' with Jesus* Christ.

Lombard 91

Lord see **Kyrios**

Lord's Day Sunday*, the day of Jesus'* Resurrection*.

Lord's Prayer 75

Lord's Supper 75

Lourdes 138

Louvre 91

Low Mass 75

Low Sunday The Sunday* after Easter Sunday*.

Lozenge 91

Lucernarium The ritual of lighting a lamp at dusk with a hymn and prayer*, which early Christians* imported into their evening prayer* as a celebration of Christ* the Light*. It survives to this day in the Vespers* rites of Spain and Milan, and has been adopted by many recently revised liturgies* also.

Luke, Gospel of Saint 108

Lych gate 91

Maccabees Books of (1, 2) 104

Magisterium 49

Magnificat 98

Magus (plural **Magi**) (Greek [from Persian] *magos* – seer, magician) A priest* of the Persian fire-religion, or more generally, a magician. See **Epiphany**

Malachi, Book of 107

Mammon (Aramaic *mammon* – riches) Wealth, especially wealth as an idol (Matthew* 6:24).

Mandatum (Latin *mandatum* – command) The title given to the washing of feet on Maundy Thursday.

Manichaean An exponent of a heresy* named after Mani the Persian (216–76CE) who maintained that from the beginning good and evil were equal and opposed, and that all matter was evil, the creation of the evil deity.

Maniple 119

Mantelletta 119

Mark, Gospel of Saint 108

Mark, Saint, Evangelist 138

Marriage, form of 151

Marriage, mixed 152

Marriage rite 58

Marriage, Sacrament of 56

Marriage tribunal 152

Martyr 138

Martyrdom 139

Martyrology 139

Mary see **Our Lady**

Mass 75

Mass, Canon of the 75

Mass, Common/Ordinary of 75

Mass, High/Low see **High Mass, Low Mass**

Mass, Nuptial 76

Mass of Oils see **Thursday, Maundy or Holy**

Mass of the Presanctified A Liturgy of the Word* with communion* from bread* previously consecrated at Mass* ('Presanctified'). The Good Friday*

Liturgy* was once described as a Mass of the Presanctified.

Mass, order of 57

Mass, Proper of 75

Mass, Requiem 77

Matins 75

Matrimonial tribunal (Latin *matrimonium* – marriage, and *tribunal* – court) See **Marriage tribunal**

Matrimony (Latin *matrimonium* – marriage) see **Marriage**

Matthew, Gospel of Saint 108

Matthew, Saint, Apostle and Evangelist 139

Maundy Thursday 65

Mediator (Latin *medius* – middle) One who stands between two opposing factions as a reconciler. In the New Testament*, Christ* is described as the Mediator between God* and humankind.

Meditation (Latin *meditare* – to repeat, to mumble) see **Prayer**

Memorial 75

Memorial, eucharistic A term for the Eucharist*, as in Jesus'* command 'Do this in memory of me' (Luke* 22:19).

Mensa 91

Mercy, Sisters of 125

Mercy, works of There are two kinds. The Spiritual works are to counsel doubters, instruct the ignorant, warn sinners*, comfort the afflicted, forgive offences, bear wrong with patience, pray for the living and dead. The Corporal works (see Matthew* 25:31–46) are: to feed the hungry, give drink to the thirsty, clothe the naked, visit those in prison, shelter the homeless, visit the sick and bury the dead.

Merit (Latin *merere* – to deserve) The blessings* gained for humanity by Christ* or the Saints*.

Messiah see **Christ**

Metropolitan 147

Metropolitan tribunal 147

Micah, Book of 107

Michael, the Archangel 139

Midday Prayer 75

Mid Lent Sunday see **Laetare Sunday, Mothering Sunday**

Military orders 125

Mind, Month's 76

Mind, Year's see **Year's Mind**

Minister 115

Minister, extraordinary of communion 115

Ministries, lay 115

Ministry, sacred/ordained 113

Miracle (Latin *miraculum* – a wonder) A happening against the laws of nature and a sign of divine presence. See **Canonisation**, **Sign**

Misericord 91

Missa (Medieval Latin *missa* – dismissal) The Latin for 'Mass'. See **Mass**

Missal 75

Mission (Latin *missio* – sending) The term usually has four uses. First is the mission of Christ*, to save the human race; second is the Church's* mission to continue that of Christ; third, the location where the gospel* is preached* and Christian* communities established. Parishes* also have missions, i.e., exercises to strengthen the faith.*

Mission architecture 91

Missionary congregations 125

Mitre 119

Mixed marriage 152

Modal 98

Mode 99

Moderator 147

Monastery 125

Monk 125

Monogram, sacred see **I.H.S.**

Monsignor (Italian *monsignore* – 'my lord') A title given by the Holy See* to clergy*. Monsignors are of three ranks, papal chaplains (lower) and prelates of honour and protonotaries apostolic (higher).

Monstrance 75

Month's Mind 76

Monument 91

Morning Prayer 76

Mortal sin (Latin *mortalis* – deadly) Serious wrongdoing, an action consciously and deliberately carried out to break God's* law.

Mortification (Latin *mortificare* – to put to death) The spiritual discipline of 'dying to self', rejecting all that turns one away from doing the will of God*.

Mosaic 91

Motet 99

Mothering Sunday An old title of the Fourth Sunday* of Lent*, referring probably to the medieval readings at Mass* for that day which referred to 'Jerusalem, the Mother of us all' (Galatians* 4:26).

Mother of God 139

Motu Proprio (Latin for 'on his own initiative') A document written at the Pope's* own initiative.

Moulding 91

Moveable feast 76

Mozzetta 120

M.R. 133

Mullion 91

Music, liturgical see the section on 'Music in the Liturgy' 96

Mystery/-ies (Greek *mysterion* – hidden thing, or ritual/dramatic action) In the Scriptures*, the term is used of God's* plan for creation and redemption*, God's 'secret' now revealed in Christ*. In theology*, it means a truth revealed* which cannot be known by reason. In liturgy*, the term is used to denote both the saving work of Christ and its enactment in the sacraments*, particularly baptism* and the Eucharist*.

Mystical body (Latin *corpus mysticum*) A term anciently used to denote the body of Christ* in the Eucharist*, but later used to denote the Church* as Christ's body.

Mysticism An experience of God in prayer*.

Nahum, Book of 107

Nails 133

Narthex 91

National conference of bishops see **Episcopal conference**

Natural law According to Church* teaching, the law which, by their very nature, all beings capable of reasoning and reflection have within themselves. It forms a basic moral code, enabling them to distinguish between right and wrong.

Nave 91

Nehemiah, Book of 103

Neo-Catechumenate Movement 125

Neophyte (Greek *neo* – new, and *physis* – nature) In sacramental* teaching, one who in baptism* has acquired a 'new' nature, through being united to the dying and rising of Christ*.

New Fire 76

New movements see **Cursillo Movement, Focolare Movement, Neo-Catechumenate Movement** and **Opus Dei**

New Testament 107

Nicene Creed 49

Night Prayer 76

Nimbus see **Halo**

None 76

Norman 91

Novena 76

Novice 126

Novitiate 126

Nullity 152

Numbers, Book of 102

Numinous (Latin *numen* – the holy)

What is experienced as 'holy'*, eliciting feelings of wonder and awe.

Nun 126

Nunc dimittis 99

Nuncio 147

Nunnery 126

Nuptial blessing 76

Nuptial Mass 76

O Antiphons 99

Obadiah, Book of 107

Oblates 126

Octave (Latin *octavus* – eighth) A period of eight days following a major solemnity*, extending the celebration. Christmas* and Easter* each have an octave.

Offertory 76

Office 76

Office, Divine 60, 71

Office hymn 99

Office of readings 76

Officialis 147

Oil of Catechumens 76

Oil of the Sick 76

Oils 76

Oils, Mass of see **Thursday, Maundy or Holy**

Old Catholics Catholic* groups in Europe who refused to subscribe to the dogma* of papal* infallibility* defined by the First Vatican* Council in 1870.

Old Testament 101

Omnipotence (Latin *omnis* – all, and *potens* – powerful) A title and attribute of God*, for whom nothing is impossible.

Omnipresence (Latin *omnis* – all, and *praesens* – present) An attribute of God, present everywhere and always.

Omniscience (Latin *omnis* – all, and *scientia* – knowledge) An attribute of God, 'all-knowing'.

Opus Dei (Latin for 'the work of God') The term used in monasteries* for the singing of the daily

office*. It originates in the Rule of Saint Benedict*.

Opus Dei (International organisation) 126

Oratorians 126

Oratorio 99

Oratory 91

Ordain/ed 115

Order, architectural 91

Order for the Baptism of Infants, 129

Order for the Dedication of a Church and Altar 129

Order of Christian Funerals 129

Order of Mass 57

Order, holy see **Holy Order**

Order, monastic 126

Order, religious 126

Orders, classical 86

Orders, military 125

Orders, Sacrament of 56

Ordinal A term used to denote the Rite of Ordination* or the books that contained it.

Ordinand 115

Ordinary 147

Ordinary, local 147

Ordinary of the Mass 76

Ordinary Time, Sundays and weekdays of 66

Ordination 113, 115

Organ 91

Original Sin (Old English *synn* – separation) In Catholic* teaching, the separation of humanity from God*, the loss of intimacy with, and alienation from, God that resulted. Genesis* 3 describes this mythically, in terms of an act of disobedience. In Catholic theology*, humanity is subject to death*, and the desire to act contrary to reason and grace*.

Orphrey 120

Orthodox Church (Greek *orthos* – right, and *doxazein* – to glorify or believe) The name given to those churches* separated from communion* with the apostolic

Orthodoxy

See*, nominally since the Great Schism* of 1054, but in fact for longer.

Orthodoxy (Greek *orthos* – right, and *doxazein* – to glorify or believe) Holding correct opinions on belief.

O Salutaris 99

Our Father The common title among Catholics* for the Lord's Prayer*.

Our Lady 136

Our Lady of Perpetual Succour see **Perpetual Succour, Our Lady of**

Padre (Spanish for 'father') A title occasionally applied to priests*, especially to military chaplains*.

Pagan (Latin *pagus* – village) One who is not a Christian* believer but an adherent of another religion. The term is not usually used of Jews or Moslems.

Pall 91

Pall, altar 83

Pall, funeral see **Funeral pall**

Palm leaves 133

Palm Sunday of the Lord's Passion 64

Panegyric (Greek *panegyrikos* – of a public assembly) A funeral speech in praise of the deceased.

Papabile (Latin *Papa* – Pope) A cardinal* or other bishop* who is thought to be a suitable candidate at the time of a papal* election.

Papacy 147

Papal (Latin *Papa* – Pope) Of or pertaining to the Pope* or his office.

Papal bull see **Bull, papal**

Papal letter see **Letter (papal) encyclical**

Parable (Greek *parabole* – a moral tale) A feature of Christ's* teaching, a story drawn from nature or human life. Parables are intended to challenge the listeners to a change of heart.

Paraclete (Greek *parakletos* – advocate) A title of the Holy Spirit*, based on John* 16:5–11. See **Advocate**

Paralipomena (Greek *para* – about, and *leipein* – to leave or omit) The Latin Vulgate* title for the two Books of Chronicles* – originating in the view that they contained what had been 'left out' of the Books of Samuel* and Kings*.

Parclose 91

Parish 147

Parish administrator 147

Parish church 148

Parish council 148

Parish priest 148

Parochial (Greek *para* – about, and *oikos* – dwelling) Of or concerning the parish*.

Parousia (Greek for 'arrival' or 'presence') The return in glory of Christ*, who will end the present world order and judge the living and dead. The early Church* believed that the parousia was imminent (cf. 1 and 2 Thessalonians*) but the Church does not speculate about the time and place of Christ's coming.

Particular Church see **Local church**

Parvis/parvise 91

Paschal (Greek, from Hebrew, *pascha* – Passover) Of or pertaining to Easter*. See also **Passover**

Paschal candle 92

Paschal duty The obligation fixed by the Fourth Lateran Council* in 1215 that Catholics* should receive Communion* once a year at Easter*.

Paschal lamb 133

Paschal mystery (Greek *pascha* – Passover, and *mysterion* – event/enactment; Latin *Mysterium Paschale*) A term central to the theological and liturgical thinking of the Second Vatican Council*. It denotes the dying and rising of Christ* and the accomplishment of that event in the sacraments* of the Church*, particularly baptism* and the Eucharist*.

Passion 64, 139

Passion, instruments of the 132

Passion Sunday see **Palm Sunday of the Lord's Passion**

Passover (Hebrew/Greek *Pascha*) The Jewish festival of liberation celebrated every spring. The festival may have originated in prehistory as a combination of a celebration of lambing and the first grain in spring. In biblical times it commemorated the death* of the Egyptian firstborn and the escape of the people of Israel from Egypt (see Exodus* 12). The people slaughtered lambs and marked their doors with the blood, so that the destroying angel* would pass over the houses of the Hebrews. The lamb was eaten with unleavened bread* as an immediate prelude to departure. Christians* thought of Christ* as a 'new' Passover sacrifice*, as he was crucified and rose at Passover time. See 1 Corinthians* 5:7–8. See entries under **Paschal**.

Pastor (Latin for 'shepherd') A title of the bishop* as chief 'shepherd' of the diocese*, also commonly given to priests*, especially (in the United States) to parish priests*.

Pastoral Of or pertaining to the non-administrative work of the bishop* or other minister* of the Church*.

Pastoral letter see **Letter, pastoral**

Pastoral letters (NT) 110

Pastoral staff 120

Paten 76

Patriarch 139

Patristics (Latin *patres* – fathers) The study of the great Christian* writers of the early Church* up to about 800CE.

Patron saint 139

Paul, Letters of Saint 109

Paul, Saint 139

Pauline privilege 152

Pax 76

Peace, sign of see **Sign of peace**

Pectoral cross 120

Pelican 133

Penance (Latin *paenitentia* – penance) An action performed in response to absolution* in the Sacrament of Penance*. A penance may include acts of charity*, prayer* or self-denial.

Penance, Sacrament of 59

Pendentive 92

Penitent 77

Penitential Rite 77

Penitentiary, apostolic 144

Penny Catechism A summary of the Catholic* faith* first published in 1899 in London. The American *Baltimore Catechism* was a similar document.

Pentateuch 101

Pentecost 65

Pericope (Greek *pericope* – portion) The name given by biblical scholars to a passage of Scripture*.

Perpendicular 92

Perpetual Succour, Our Lady of An ancient icon* of Our Lady* and the child Jesus*, in which the child, frightened by angels* displaying the instruments of the Passion*, is comforted by his mother. The original is now in Rome.

Person (Latin *persona*) see **Trinity**

Peter, Basilica of, Saint (Vatican Basilica) Over the site of Saint Peter's* grave*, the Emperor Constantine built a basilica* in the fourth century

CE. This was replaced in the fifteenth century by the present basilica, designed by Michelangelo and completed in the seventeenth century. It is associated with the Pope*, who since the fifteenth century has resided in the Vatican* Palace next to Saint Peter's.

Peter's Pence The annual worldwide collection taken at the feast* of Saint Peter* and Paul* (29 June) to support the Holy See*.

Petition (Latin *petere* – to seek or ask) The prayer* in which God* is asked to grant requests.

Petto, in (Italian for 'in the heart', i.e., secretly) The appointment of a cardinal* which, for political sensitivity, is not made public.

Piety (Latin *pietas* – dutiful or filial affection) A gift of the Holy Spirit*, which fosters love of parents and family. The term is also used of certain devotional acts, such as the veneration of saints*.

Pilgrim/pilgrimage (Latin *peregrinus* – wanderer, stranger) One who journeys to a holy* place for religious* reasons. The word is also used in the liturgy* as an image of the Christian* life as a journey.

Pontiff, Roman see **Roman pontiff**

Power of Keys see **Keys, power of**

Prague, Infant of A statue of the infant Jesus*, elaborately robed and crowned, given to the Church* of Our Lady of Victory in Prague in 1628. It is a popular image for devotion* to the childhood of Jesus.

Prayer (Latin *prex* – an earnest or solemn prayer) The activity of placing heart, mind and body in conversation and relationship with God*. Christian* prayer rests on the conviction that God is accessible; that though God is the source of all being, God is also Father*; that the Father has sent his eternal Son* Jesus* Christ* to free us from death* and alienation from God, and that he sends the Holy Spirit* to those who believe, to complete Christ's work on earth and bring believers to share the fullness of God's life as Trinity*. Prayer is made in many ways. It may be liturgical*, as in all Christian worship*, or personal; it may be out loud or silent; it may be a bodily act such as lighting a candle* or making the sign of the cross*. Prayer is often made with Scripture*, as in the meditative reading from the Bible* known as 'Lectio divina'* (literally, 'holy reading'); it may be 'contemplative', without words or text. Christian tradition* is that prayer has to be learnt, and that Christ taught the Church* to pray by his example, and by teaching the Our Father* or Lord's Prayer* as a pattern for all prayers.

Prayer, bidding 68

Prayer, Evening 72

Prayer, Lord's see **Our Father**

Prayer, Morning 76

Prayer of quiet see **Quiet, prayer of**

Prayer over the gifts, Prayer after communion 58

Prayer rope 77

Preach/er/ing (Latin *praedicare* – to proclaim) To deliver a homily* at Mass* or a sermon*; the minister* who delivers it.

Precentor 99

Precepts of the Church see **Commandments of the Church**

Predella 92

Preface 77

Preface, Proper 77

Prelate 148

Presanctified, Mass of the see **Mass of the Presanctified**

Presbyter 115

Presbyterate 116

Presbytery 148

Presence, real 77

Presentation of the Lord, Feast of the 66

Pricket 92

Prie-Dieu 92

Priest 114, 116

Priest, assistant 144

Priest, parish 148

Priesthood 116

Priest-in-charge 148

Priests, council of 146

Primate 148

Prime 77

Prior 126

Priory 126

Privilege, Pauline 152

Privilege, Petrine 152

Procession 77

Processional cross 92

Profession of faith 77

Profession, religious 126

Promises, baptismal 68

Promoter of the faith 148

Promulgate To issue and give effect to an important document in the Church*.

Propaganda Fide (propagation of the faith) 148

Proper (Latin *proprium* – belonging to) Those parts of a service* that are special for certain occasions.

Proper of the Mass 77

Proper Preface 77

Prophet (Greek *prophetes* – one who speaks out or foretells) The Old Testament* prophets were speakers of God's* word* and judgements* on the people of Israel and Judah. They flourished from the time of the divided kingdoms (*c*.9th century BCE) until the exile (6th century BCE) and after. The term is used more generally to refer to all the great figures of the Old Testament, such as Moses and Samuel.

Propitiation (Latin *propitiare* – to appease or gain the favour of someone) Reconciliation*. The understanding that Christ* has reconciled us to God* the Father* through his sacrifice* (see 1 John* 2:1).

Protestant The self-definition of the Reformers in the sixteenth century as 'protesting' against the abuses of the Roman Church*. See **Reformation, Protestant**

Protonotary apostolic see **Monsignor**

Proverbs, Book of 104

Providence (Latin prefix *pro* – forward, and *videre* – to see) An attribute of God*, who sees and cares for everything in the creation.

Province 126

Provincial 126

Provost (Latin *praepositus* – in charge) The senior priest* of a cathedral* chapter*.

Psalm 99

Psalmody 99

Psalm prayer 77

Psalm, responsorial see **Responsorial psalm**

Psalms, Book of 104

Psalter 99

Pulpit 92

Punishment, temporal see **Temporal punishment**

Purgatory (Latin *purgare* – to cleanse) The state of those believers who have died at rights with God*, but remain in need of purification. The medieval Italian poet Dante envisaged Purgatory as a happy place, because those within it were assured of redemption*. See **All Souls**, **Eschatology**

Purificator 77

Purlin 92

Purse 133

Putative 152

Pyx 92

Pyx, hanging 90

Q (German *Quelle* – source) In New Testament* study, the presumed source for material common to the Gospels* of Matthew* and Luke*, possibly composed in Antioch about 50CE.

Quiet, prayer of A form of prayer*, the first stage of mystical prayer or prayer of union with God*.

Quietism A seventeenth-century heresy* of complete passivity before God*, which taught that for those who have submitted their will to God, anything they do, whether good or evil, is of no account before God.

Quinquagesima (Latin for 'fiftieth [day]') The name formerly given to the Second Sunday* before Lent*. The term was abolished in the reforms after the Second Vatican Council*.

Quoin 92

Rafter 93

Rails, altar 83

Ratified 152

Reader 116

Readings, Office of 76

Real presence 77

Recollection A general term covering prayer*. Days of retreat* or prayer are sometimes known as 'Days of Recollection'.

Reconciliation Re-establishing a damaged relationship. Christ*, in Catholic* teaching, has reconciled humans to the Father* (see 2 Corinthians* 4:17–19).

Reconciliation, Eucharistic Prayers of Two special Eucharistic Prayers* issued by the Holy See* in 1975 to mark the Holy Year.

Rector 148

Rectory 148

Redeemer (Latin *redemptor* – one who buys back or redeems/ransoms) A title of Christ*, who 'redeemed' creation from its slavery to sin* by the paschal mystery*.

Redemption (Latin *redemptio* – buying back/ransoming) The name given to the saving death* and Resurrection of Christ*. See **Redeemer**.

Redundant church see **Church, redundant**

Refectory 126

Reformation, Catholic The name sometimes given to the Council of Trent* (1545–69) and the reforms that accompanied it in the sixteenth century, in response to the Protestant Reformation*.

Reformation, Protestant The term given to the split in the Catholic* Church* of the sixteenth century and the schism* associated with the names of Martin Luther, John Calvin and Ulrich Zwingli. They taught that Scripture* was the only source for teaching, that every person had the right to interpret and use the Bible*, that faith* alone and not religious* practice put people at rights with God*. In England, the Reformation began as a break with the Holy See* under Henry VIII, and only later, with the ascendancy of the Protestants* at Court and the introduction of the *Book of Common Prayer* in 1549, became a doctrinal* and liturgical* split. The Anglican* Church* sought to pursue a middle way by taking the best from both Catholic and Protestant traditions*. The English Reformation is now more usually perceived as a movement initially inspired by the Tudor state which only slowly received the assent of the populace.

Regeneration, baptismal (Latin *regenerare* – to give new life) The rebirth enacted in baptism* (see Romans* 6).

Registers 148

Relic 93

Religion (Latin *religare* – to bind) The group of beliefs and practices by which human beings engage with the transcendent God*. In Catholic* teaching, religion is a moral virtue that expresses itself in worship* and service of God.

Religious 126

Religious profession 126

Reliquary 93

Remembrance Sunday 67

Remission (Latin *remittere* – to remit) The forgiveness of sins*.

Rendering 93

Renovation 93

Renunciation (baptism) 77

Re-ordering 93

Repentance (Latin *paenitentia* – penitence) The act of being sorry for one's sins*, accompanied by a desire to change. See **Penance, Sacrament of**

Repose, altar of 83

Requiem Mass 77

Reredos 93

Reservation, Blessed Sacrament 77

Response 99

Responsorial 99

Responsorial psalm 99

Responsory 99

Resurrection (Latin *resurgere* – to rise again) The term describing the rising of Christ* from the dead (see Mark* 16:1–7.) It is the central doctrine* of the Church* (see 1 Corinthians* 15:13–58) and the guarantee of the believer's resurrection with Christ through the Sacrament* of Baptism* (see Romans* 6:5–8). The Resurrection of Christ is celebrated every Sunday*, and annually with a three days' celebration from Holy Thursday* evening until Easter Sunday* evening.

Resurrection of the body The belief expressed in the Scriptures* (Philippians* 3:20–21) and articulated in the creeds*, that the body of believers will be transformed and raised up as a spiritual being in company with the Risen Christ*. See **Resurrection**

Retable 93

Retreat A period of prayer* and reflection, usually involving a stay in a religious* house or special retreat centre. Retreats are sometimes termed 'Spiritual Exercises'* though this is, strictly speaking, a feature of Jesuit* religious* life.

Retreatant One who goes on retreat*.

Reveal 93

Revelation, Book of see **Apocalypse**

Revelation, divine The self-communication of God* to humankind. This revelation is found in the history of God's dealings with his people, the 'Word' and tradition attested to by the Scriptures*, culminating in Christ*, the Incarnate* Word, who in his person, works and teaching represents the fullness of revelation. The truths of revelation are communicated to us through the Scriptures* and in the teaching of the Church*.

Reverend 148

Rib 93

Riddel 93

Ring 120

R.I.P. 133

Rite 77

Rite of Anointing and Pastoral Care of the Sick 129

Rite for the Christian Initiation of Adults (R.C.I.A.) 129

Rite of Confirmation 129

Rite of Election 77

Rite, Funeral 61

Rite of Marriage 129

Rite of Ordination 129

Rite of Penance 129

Ritual 78, 129

Robe, seamless see **Seamless robe**

Rochet 120

Rogations (Latin *rogare* – to ask) Days during the spring when fasting was customary. At one time the 'rogations' were celebrated on 25 April as days of prayer* for crops. This practice was discontinued in the Roman Missal* of 1969.

Roman Catholics A term used since the seventeenth century by English Catholics to describe themselves as compared to others, such as Anglicans*, who also consider themselves as belonging

to the Catholic* Church*. Outside England the term is more rarely used.

Roman Curia 148

Roman pontiff (Latin *pontifex* – bridge-builder) A title of the Pope* as Bishop* of Rome. In pagan* Rome, the chief priest* of the state religion* was known as 'Pontifex Maximus' and had the charge, among other things, of maintaining the bridges over the Tiber, which were regarded as sacred structures. The title was later assumed by the popes as a sign of their civic responsibility.

Roman pontifical 129

Roman Rite 78

Roman ritual 129

Roman rota 149

Romanesque 93

Romans, Saint Paul's Letter to the 109

Rome/See of Rome, Holy see **Holy See**

Rood 93

Rood loft 93

Rood screen 93

Roof, saddle 93

Roof, wagon 95

Rosary 78

Rose 133

Rose window 93

Rubric 78

Rule 127

Rule of Saint Benedict 127

Ruth, Book of 102

Sabaoth The title given to God* by the Seraphim* in Isaiah* 6:3: 'Lord of Sabaoth'. The meaning of the Hebrew is unclear. It may mean 'hosts' in the military sense, or refer to the 'heavenly host' of stars, or angelic beings. It forms part of the Sanctus* in the Eucharistic Prayer*.

Sabbath (Hebrew *Shabbath*) Saturday, the Jewish Holy* Day. The

Old Testament* gives two accounts of its institution. In Exodus* 20:11; 31:17 it represents God's* rest after creation; in Deuteronomy* 5:15 it is kept as a day in remembrance of the deliverance from slavery. Strict laws forbade work on the Sabbath. Jesus* protested against the over-zealous interpretation of Sabbath rest. Early Christians* transferred their 'holy day' to Sunday*, the day of Christ's* Resurrection* (see **Lord's Day**), though some Christian traditions still celebrate Saturday as a day of celebration.

Sacrament 55

Sacrament, Blessed 77

Sacrament house 93

Sacramental (Latin *sacramentale* – like a sacrament) A sacred act or object involved in liturgy*, such as the Ash Wednesday* ashes, holy water*, palms on Palm Sunday* and the washing of feet* on Holy Thursday*.

Sacramental confession see **Sacrament of Penance**

Sacramental form 72

Sacramentary (Latin *Liber Sacramentorum*) A name given in the early Middle Ages to the books and collections of prayers* for the bishop* or priest* to use at Mass* and other services*. With the addition of readings and other things in the tenth century and after, the larger book known as the Missal* came into being.

Sacrarium 93

Sacred Heart The representation of the heart of Jesus* pierced on the left side, or with five wounds, was an object of devotion* from the late Middle Ages. It became in the seventeenth century a symbol of God's* love for humankind and of redemption* through

Christ's* Passion*. Catholics* still practise special acts of prayer* to the Sacred Heart and it is a common dedication* title for Catholic* churches*.

Sacred Heart of Jesus, Solemnity of the 66

Sacred ministry see **Ministry, sacred/ordained**

Sacred monogram see **I.H.S.**

Sacred Triduum of the Passion and Resurrection of the Lord 64

Sacred vessels 93

Sacrifice 78

Sacrilege (Latin *sacra* – holy things, and *legere* – to take or steal) The theft or abuse of a dedicated* building or object.

Sacristan 78

Sacristy 93

Saddle roof 93

Saint Andrew 137

Saint Anna 137

Saint John the Baptist 138

Saint Mark 138

Saint Matthew 139

Saint, patron 139

Saint Paul 139

Saint Paul, Letters of 109

Saint Peter 139

Saints 135

Saints, All 136

Saints, Litany of the 74

Saltire 133

Salvation (Latin *salus* – health, safety) In Christian usage, the liberation from death* and sin* and entry into eternal* life through the paschal mystery* of Christ*, effected for believers through faith*, the Church* and the sacraments*.

Salve Regina 99

Samuel, Books of (1, 2) 103

Sanctification (Latin *sanctus* – holy, and *facere* – to make) Being made holy*. Holiness is the nature and gift of God*, supremely shown and enacted for humans in Christ* and communicated to humans through Christ in the Church*, by the agency of the Holy Spirit*. Ultimately, sanctification is a sharing in the life of the Trinity*. While holiness is a gift, it is something for which Christian* teaching urges believers to strive.

Sanctifier (Latin *sanctificator* – the one who makes holy) A title of the Holy Spirit*.

Sanctuary 93

Sanctuary step 93

Sanctus 100

Sanctus bell 78

Sanctus candle 78

Satan (Hebrew *satan* – adversary) A title for the personification of evil in the Old* and New Testaments*.

Saturday, Holy 65

Saviour (Latin *salvator* – one who saves) The title of Christ*. See **Atonement**, **Salvation**

Scallop shell 133

Scapular 127

Schism (Greek *schisma* – split, rent) A breach in the unity* of the Church*.

Scholasticism The term given to the predominant medieval philosophy and theology*, found in the writings of Saint Thomas Aquinas (page 140) and others, which employed the philosophy of Aristotle as an inspiration.

Sconce 93

Screen 93

Scripture (Latin *scripta* – things written) The Bible*; the written word* of God* inspired by the Holy Spirit*. Scripture consists of the Old Testament* and the new Testament. The Old Testament consists of the Jewish *Torah* or Law, which is contained in the Pentateuch* or first five books of the Old Testament. This is followed by historical, lyrical and prophetic books. The New Testament comprises the four Gospels*, the Acts of the Apostles*, the Letters* and the Book of Revelation*.

Scripture, Canon of see **Canon of Scripture**

Scrutinies 78

Seamless robe 134

Season 62

Second Coming see **Parousia**

Second instance, tribunal of see **Roman rota**

Second Vatican Council 51

Secular (Latin *saeculum* – generation, age) Pertaining to this world; usually employed as the opposite of 'religious'*.

Secular institute While not religious* orders* secular institutes are groups of Christian* people who, while living ordinary working lives, make vows and practise poverty, chastity and obedience.

Sede vacante (Latin for 'vacant chair') The interregnum between office holders. Often used of the Pope* and bishops*.

Sedelia 93

See see Holy See and 144

Seminary (Latin *seminarium* – a place to sow seeds) A college where priests* are trained. In the Middle Ages the training of priests was haphazard. The Council of Trent* ordered reform of the system, evolving the seminary as a combination of university and religious* house. Each diocese* was to have its own seminary. Nowadays seminaries are organised on a national or multi-diocesan basis and the training of clergy* takes place in parishes* as well as in seminaries.

Separated Eastern Churches see **Eastern Churches, Separated**

Septuagesima (Latin for 'the seventieth' day) The title formerly given to the third week before Lent* and to the Sunday* occurring at the start of that week.

Septuagint (Latin *septuaginta* – seventy) The Greek version of the Old Testament* including the Apocryphal books, said to have been made in Alexandria in the third century BCE by translation from the Hebrew, the work of seventy translators. The Septuagint is the Old Testament text on which the Vulgate* and Catholic* Bibles* generally are based.

Sequence 99

Seraphim According to Isaiah* 6:3, heavenly beings made of fire, with six wings, hovering before the presence of God* and shouting 'Holy, Holy, Holy* Lord of Sabaoth*'. The details are probably inspired by Assyrian depictions of guardian spirits. In medieval thought, the seraphim ranked as the superior order of angels*.

Sermon 78

Server 78

Services, church Ritual activity. See **Liturgy**

Sexagesima (Latin for 'sixtieth') The title formerly given to the second week before Lent* and the Sunday* that occurred in that week.

Sext 79

Shaft 93

Shell, baptismal 85

Shell, scallop 133

Ship 134

Shrine 93

Shrines of Our Lady in Great Britain 140

Shroud of Turin An ancient linen cloth, kept in Turin Cathedral, with a human image somehow imprinted upon the cloth. It is claimed by tradition* to be the burial* cloth of Jesus*, though recent dating has revealed it to be of medieval manufacture.

Shrove Tuesday (Old English *shriven* – having been to confession*) The day before Ash Wednesday*. It is also known as Pancake Day because of the use of certain foods such as eggs and butter, at one time forbidden during the fasting season of Lent*. It was therefore necessary to eat them up on this day.

Sick, see **Anointing of the Sick, Sacrament of, and Oil of the Sick**

Sign A term with various uses in Christian teaching. In the New Testament, particularly in the Gospel of John*, it is used to denote the miracles* of Jesus*, as signs by which he showed his glory. In theology* a sacrament* is a sign that effects what it signifies.

Sign of the cross see **Cross, sign of the**

Sign of peace 79

Signatura, apostolic 144

Simony 149

Sin/Sinner (Old English *synn, sunder* – to break) A choice in favour of evil and against God*, which harms or even breaks the bond of friendship with God. See **Mortal sin** and **Original Sin**

Sisters 127

Skull and crossbones 134

Slype 93

Sodality (Latin *sodalitas* – companionship) The name given to many associations and societies in the Church* which exist to promote particular types of prayer*, spirituality or pastoral action.

Soffit 94

Solemnity 79

Solesmes 100

Son, God the The Second Person

of the Trinity*, who was incarnate* of the Virgin Mary* and born as Jesus* of Nazareth, named Christ* or Messiah by believers.

Song of Solomon, Book of the 105

Soul That element of human personhood that animates the body and activities such as remembering, thinking and willing. Each human soul is individually created by God*.

Sounding board 94

Spandrel 94

Spear 134

Species 79

Spire 94

Spirit, Holy see **Holy Spirit**

Spiritual director One who acts as a guide to others in teaching prayer and supporting their spiritual life.

Spiritual direction see **Direction, spiritual**

Spiritual Exercises see **Retreat**

Sponsor (Latin *spondere* – to promise) One who presents a person for baptism* or confirmation* and undertakes a responsibility for that person's spiritual growth. In Catholic* practice, sponsors should themselves have been baptised and confirmed, and be regular attenders at Mass*. See **Baptismal sponsor**.

Staff, pastoral 120

Stained glass 94

Stall 94

Stations of the Cross 94

Steeple 94

Step, sanctuary 93

Steward, stewardship (Old English *stiweard* – a housekeeper) An idea from Scripture*, whereby humans are given the world in trust by God* to look after, and will have to render an account of how they have done this. The term is also often used of campaigns for fundraising.

Stigmata (Greek *stigma* – wound or mark) Marks on the hands, feet and side resembling those of Christ* on the cross*. Saint Francis of Assisi suffered the appearance of these marks towards the end of his life. They are said to be a sign of holiness.

Stipend 149

Stole 120

Stole fees 149

Stoup 94

String course 94

Stucco 94

Subdeacon 116

Substance In medieval philosophy, after Aristotle, the essence of something as distinguished from its outward appearance. The term is used in connection with the Eucharist* to denote the reality of Christ's* body and blood*, and in connection with the theology* of the Trinity* where the persons, the Father*, Son* and Spirit*, are distinguished from their substance, or divinity.

Succession, apostolic see **Apostolic Succession**

Successor of Saint Peter see **Pope**

Suffragan bishop 149

Sunday 62

Sunday, Gaudete see **Gaudete Sunday**

Sunday, Low see **Low Sunday**

Sunday, Laetare see **Laetare Sunday**

Sunday, Mid Lent see **Laetare Sunday**

Sunday, Mothering Another name for the Fourth Sunday* of Lent*. See **Laetare Sunday**

Sunday, Palm 64

Sunday, Passion see **Palm Sunday of the Lord's Passion**

Sunday, Remembrance 67

Sunday, Trinity see **Holy Trinity, Solemnity of the**

Sunday, Whit see **Pentecost**

Sundays of Advent 62

Sundays of Easter see **Easter Sunday** and **Eastertime**

Sundays of Lent 63

Sundays of Ordinary Time 66

Superior 127

Supper, the Lord's A title for the Eucharist*.

Supplication (Latin *supplex* – one who begs) A term used to denote earnest and sustained prayer* in the liturgy*.

Surplice 120

Suspension 149

Sword 134

Symbol (Greek *syn* – with, and *balein* – to throw) In Christian* theology* a symbol is a sign* of a special kind. It is an action or thing that connects with what is symbolised, described or alluded to by the symbol. Symbols, in other words, effect what they signify. It is close in meaning to the term 'sacrament'*.

Synaxis (Greek for 'assembly') The term given to denote any liturgical rite*.

Synod 149

Synoptic Gospels 108

Synoptic problem The debate over the relationship between the Gospels* of Matthew*, Mark* and Luke*, as to which is the oldest and how much of the content of one is reproduced in the other. See **Synoptic Gospels**

Tabernacle 94

Tabernacle work 94

Table, credence see **Credence**

Table, holy 73

Tablet 94

Taize 100

Tantum ergo 100

Te Deum laudamus 100

Temporal (Latin *temporale* – of time) In the liturgical* books, the collection of prayer* texts for the Church's year*, as distinct from those for saints'* days.

Temporal punishment (Latin *tempus* – time) In Church* teaching, the expiation* still to be undergone for sins* already forgiven. It is usually associated with Purgatory*.

Temptation (Latin *temptatio* – testing) Incitment to sin*. Temptation in itself is not sinful.

Ten Commandments The first part of the Book of the Covenant* in Exodus* 20; ten precepts concerning service of God* and behaviour towards other people.

Tenebrae 79

Terce 79

Testament (Latin *testamentum&* – will or witness) The title for the Bible*: Old* and New Testament*. The term is used to describe the covenant* or relationship between God* and the people.

Tester 94

Theologian (Greek *theos* – God, and *logos* – reasoning) One who practises theology*.

Theological virtues Faith*, Hope* and Charity*, as outlined in 1 Corinthians* 13.

Theology (Greek *Theos* – God, and *logos* – thought or reasoning) The science of God* and what relates to God's being and activity. A study of what is revealed* and accepted by believers. Various disciplines of theology are practised: fundamental (the nature of God), dogmatic* (salvation*) and moral (the science of Christian* ethics). See also **Dogmatic theology**

Thessalonians, Saint Paul's Letters to the (1, 2) 110

Thomas Aquinas, Saint 140
Thorns, crown of 131
Throne 94
Throne, exposition see **Throne**
Thurible 79
Thurifer 79
Thursday, Maundy or Holy 65
Tie beam 85
Tile, encaustic 89
Timothy, Saint Paul's Letters to
   (1, 2) 111
Titus, Saint Paul's Letter to 111
Tobit, Book of 103
Tomb 94
Tomb, empty see **Easter**
Tone 100
Tonsure (Latin *tonsura*) The shaving
   of the crown of the head. Origin-
   ally, monks* and clergy* were
   tonsured. The tonsure is not usu-
   ally given nowadays, though it is
   still found in some monasteries.
Towel, lavabo 74
Tower 94
Tracery 94
Tract 100
Tradition (Latin *tradere* – to hand
   on) According to Church* teaching, Scripture* and tradition together form the one source of
   revealed* truth.
Transcendence (Latin prefix *trans*
   – beyond, and *scandere* – to
   climb) The quality proper to
   God*, in that God is beyond any
   human imagining, speech or
   thought.
Transept 94
Transfiguration (Latin prefix *trans*
   – change, and *figura* – form) As
   recorded in Matthew* 17:1–3,
   Mark* 9:2–13 and Luke* 9:28–
   36; Jesus* revealed* himself as
   Son* of God* to his disciples*
   before his Passion*. The Transfiguration is kept as a liturgical*
   feast* on 6 August, and the Gospel* is read every year on the
   Second Sunday* of Lent*.

Transom 94
Transubstantiation 79
Trent, Council of 51
Trespass (Old French *trepasser* – to
   pass over) In the Lord's Prayer*,
   the term is used to mean 'sins'*.
Tribunal, appeal 151
Tribunal, marriage 152
Tribunal, metropolitan 152
Tridentine Mass 79
Triforium 94
Trinitarian Of or pertaining to the
   Holy Trinity* or faith in the
   Trinity.
Trinity (Latin *Trinitas*) God* reveals
   his inner life as the basis of his
   activity in sending the Son* and
   also the Holy Spirit*. The Christ-
   ian* faith* understands the One
   God as being in three 'persons'
   of the Father*, Son and Spirit.
Trinity Sunday see **Holy Trinity,
   Solemnity of the**
Triptych 94
Trope 100
Truss 94
Tunicle 120
Tuscan order 94
Tympanum 95

Unbaptised In Catholic* teaching,
   baptism* is necessary for obtaining eternal* life with God*;
   however, those who are not baptised are not necessarily deprived
   of God's mercy and love. Indeed,
   the Holy Innocents, the children
   killed by Herod (see Matthew*
   2:16–18), were not baptised, and
   yet are celebrated as martyrs* of
   Christ.
Unction see **Anointing of the Sick,
   Sacrament of**
Undercroft 95
Unity, Christian See **Ecumenism**
Unleavened bread 80

Valid (Latin *valere* – to have strength)
   The term used to denote a proper

and authentic celebration of a sacrament*. It is particularly used in connection with marriage*.

Validation 152

Validity 152

Vane 95

Vatican (Latin *Mons Vaticanus* – the Vatican Hill) The hill across the Tiber from the ancient city of Rome, where the racing stadium stood where, according to tradition*, the Apostle* Peter* was crucified in or about 65CE. The Emperor Constantine built the Basilica* of Saint Peter's, known as the Vatican Basilica, on the site as a pilgrimage* church* with Saint Peter's reputed grave* in its midst. Saint Peter's was rebuilt in the sixteenth and seventeenth centuries. The Vatican has been the residence of the Pope* since the fifteenth century.

Vatican II see **Second Vatican Council**

Vatican Basilica see **Peter, Basilica of**

Vault 95

Vault, barrel 85

Vault, fan 89

Vault, rib 93

Vaulting, lierne 91

Veil 80, 127

Veil, chalice see **Chalice veil**

Veil, humeral see **Humeral veil**

Veil, Lenten see **Lenten veil**

Venerable 149

Veni Creator 100

Verse 100

Versicles and responses 100

Vesica 95

Vespers 80

Vestments 120

Vestry 95

Viaticum 80

Vicar 149

Vicar, episcopal 146

Vicar forane 149

Vicar general 149

Vicar, judicial 147

Vice-officialis 149

Vigil 80

Vigil, Easter 65

Vigils 80

Virgin 127, 140

Virgin, Blessed see **Blessed Virgin Mary**

Virgin birth The Catholic* teaching that Christ* was conceived and born of Mary*, who was and remained a virgin*.

Virtues, theological see **Theological virtues**

Visitation 149

Visitor 120

Vocation 116

Votive (Latin *votum* – vow) Describing an offering or action made as a prayer* or religious* act. See **Candles**

Voussoir 95

Vulgate (Latin *vulgata* – in common speech) The Latin (common speech in the ancient Western world) version of Scripture* compiled by Saint Jerome in the Fourth Century, using earlier versions and other sources, which remained standard in the Catholic* liturgy*, with a revision of 1592 ordered by the Council of Trent*. The Vulgate was revised extensively after the Second Vatican Council.

Wafer 80

Wagon roof 95

Wake 80

Wall plate 95

Washing of the feet see **Feet, washing of**

Water 80

Water, baptismal 68

Water, holy 73

Way of the Cross see **Stations of the Cross**

Wear, clerical see **Clerical dress**

Weathercock 95

Women, churching Childbirth was held to set a woman apart from the parish* community, and the ceremony of churching marked her reappearance in the parish. In modern Catholic* practice this ritual has been abolished and a special blessing* is given to the mother at the baptism* of a child.

Word In Scripture*, God's* way of communicating with created beings. Creation itself is ascribed to the word of God (Genesis* 1); the Prophets* received and spoke God's word. In Hebrew, the term had connotations of 'event' or act of God. In Christian* teaching, Jesus* Christ* is the 'Word made flesh' (John* 1:14).

Works of mercy see **Corporal works of mercy**

Worship A term denoting the giving of praise (worth-ship) to God*. See **Liturgy**

Worship, Disparity of see **Disparity of worship**

Yahweh The personal name of God* revealed* to Moses. Jews and Christians* regard it as too sacred to be spoken. In Hebrew, only the consonants J.H.W.H. are written. The meaning is 'I am what I am', which may be either a reference to God's self-revelation through what he does; or a riddle; or (as interpreted in Greek) 'I am who am' – the 'fullness of being'. See **Jehovah**

Year's Mind A term for the anniversary of a death*, often the occasion for a Mass* for the repose of the soul* of the dead person.

PART TWO

THE TEACHING CHURCH

CREEDS AND COUNCILS

1 The Creeds

'Creed' comes from Latin *Credo*, 'I believe'. It is a summary statement of faith*. The creed originates in the ancient baptism* rite. As candidates were baptised the bishop* asked them three questions: 'Do you believe in God* the Father*?' 'Do you believe in Jesus* Christ*?' 'Do you believe in the Holy Spirit*?' To each of these questions the candidate answered 'I believe' and was baptised after each answer.

There are two creeds in use in the Catholic* Church*, the so-called 'Apostles' Creed' and the creed of the fourth-century Councils* of Nicaea* and Constantinople*, known simply as the 'Nicene Creed*'.

The Apostles' Creed is the simplest and is an elaboration of the questions asked at baptism. It was probably in use as a creed in the Roman Church by *c.*150CE and took on its present shape in the eighth century. This creed may be used at Mass*.

The Nicene Creed is more elaborate and theological*. It seems to have been based on the baptismal creed of the Jerusalem Church. It was formulated in the fourth century as the Church attempted to define *who* and *what* Christ was, in the face of the Arian heresy* which denied his divinity. The creed of the Council of Nicaea (which met in 325CE) was amended by the Council of Constantinople in 381CE. The Nicene Creed is recited at Sunday* Mass. Latin-speaking churches* adopted a form of the text containing the word *Filioque** that the Holy Spirit 'proceeded' from both the Father and the Son. The Eastern Churches* have never used this form, believing that the Spirit 'proceeds' from the Father alone.

The 'Athanasian' Creed, not now used, is named after Saint Athanasius, the fourth-century bishop* and theologian*. It is in fact not his, since it refutes a heresy that dates from after his time, namely that Jesus was divine but not fully human. This creed is a detailed exposition of the theology* of the Trinity*. It is almost certainly Franco-Spanish and of the early fifth century CE.

2 The Magisterium

Christ* commanded the apostles* to 'Go and teach all nations' (Matthew* 28:19, 20). The 'Magisterium' (from Latin *magister* – teacher) or teaching authority of the Church* rests on this command. It is vested in the Pope* as the successor of Saint Peter* and in the bishops* in association with the Pope.

THE TEACHING CHURCH

Some Church* teaching is known as *Ex cathedra** (Latin for 'From the [bishop's] chair) or *infallible*. Infallibility* (from Latin for 'something that does not deceive') means that the Church teaches what Christ* teaches. Such teaching demands the assent of the whole Church. Other teaching, though not 'infallible', is of high authority.

Infallible teaching (dogma*) is found in the creeds* of the Church and in affirmations of faith* defined by ecumenical councils* – and by the Pope himself, explicitly, on rare occasions. Authoritative teaching is found in major papal* letters or encyclicals*.

From the beginning the bishops of the Church met in council* to debate important matters of belief and practice. The Acts of the Apostles* records one such meeting about whether Gentile* converts should become circumcised Jews first (Acts 15). The first 'ecumenical' council, called at Nicaea, took place in 325CE.

In Catholic* teaching, ecumenical councils must always have the participation and affirmation of the Pope, either personally or by a representative. The Church sees such councils as an assembly of bishops as the successors of the apostles. The list of ecumenical councils given below gives the name of the Pope (who was not always personally present at the council) at the time, and then the Roman emperor, where appropriate.

The first eight councils listed below are regarded by Catholics*, Orthodox* and Anglicans* as ecumenical and their decisions binding. According to Roman Catholic teaching the following twenty-one councils are recognised as 'ecumenical'.

Nicaea 1 (Pope Sylvester I and Emperor Constantine) Three hundred bishops* met between spring and autumn 325CE at Nicaea (modern Iznik, in Turkey) to determine questions relating to the divinity of Christ*. The Arian heresy*, which denied his divinity, was refuted. The creed* known as the 'Nicene' Creed* was first formulated at this council. Nicaea evolved a formula for determining the date of Easter*.

Constantinople 1 (Pope Damasus I and Emperor Theodosius I) Held in the spring of 381CE, with *c*.150 bishops*, it condemned Arianism, and Macedonianism, which denied the divinity of the Holy Spirit*.

Ephesus (Pope Celestine I and Emperor Theodosius II) Held by about 200 bishops* in the summer of 431CE, to determine further questions concerning the divinity of Christ* and condemn the heresy* of Nestorianism, which denied the unity of Christ's human and divine natures. It allowed the title 'Mother of God' for the Blessed Virgin Mary*. It condemned Pelagianism, a heresy which taught that man is capable of salvation* through free will.

Chalcedon (Pope Leo I and Emperor Marcian) A meeting of about 600 bishops* in the autumn of 451CE at Chalcedon (in Turkey) to debate the Monophysite heresy*, which denied the humanity of Christ*. Pope* Leo the First's *Letter to Flavian* formed a basis for the Council's definition of the two natures, human and divine, united in the person of Christ.

Constantinople 2 (Pope Vigilius and Emperor Justinian I) Held in the spring of 553CE and attended by 165 bishops*. It met to condemn various heresies* relating to Nestorianism (See **Ephesus**).

Constantinople 3 (Pope Agatho and Emperor Leo II) Attended by about 170 bishops* from the autumn of 680 until that of 681, It condemned the heresy* of Monothelitism, which claimed that Christ* had only one (divine) will.

Nicaea 2 (Pope Adrian I and Empress Irene) A meeting of approximately 300 bishops*, held between September and October of 787. The Council was called to discuss the legitimacy of images* in church*. The Iconoclast heresy* (the belief that the Ten Commandments* forbade images) had split the Church* in the East and caused much civil unrest. The council decided in favour of images.

Constantinople 4 (Pope Adrian II and Emperor Basil I) A meeting of about 100 bishops*, held between October 859 and February 870. It condemned Iconoclasm (see **Nicaea 2**) a second time. This was the last Ecumenical Council held in the Eastern Church*.

Lateran 1 (Pope Callistus II) Held in the spring of 1123, it consisted of some 300 bishops*. Made rules for the appointment of bishops and others.

Lateran 2 (Pope Innocent II) Held in April 1139, with some 900 bishops*, it established that to be ordained* is an impediment* to marriage*.

Lateran 3 (Pope Alexander III) Held in March 1179 and attended by about 300 bishops*, it enacted measures against heresies* in France and Italy, and fixed the system of electing a Pope*.

Lateran 4 (Pope Innocent III) Sessions held in November 1215. This council defined the dogma* of Transubstantiation* and decreed that Catholics* should receive the sacraments* of Penance* and the Eucharist* at least once a year at Easter*.

Lyons 1 (Pope Innocent IV) Held in November 1245 by approximately 150 bishops*, it confirmed the deposition of the Emperor Frederick II.

Lyons 2 (Pope Gregory X) Held in the spring of 1274, with about 500 bishops*, it established (temporary) reunion between Eastern and Western Churches* and issued regulations concerning papal* election.

Vienne (Pope Clement V) Sessions between October 1311 and May 1312, attended by 132 bishops*. It suppressed the Order* of Knights Templar.

Constance (Popes Gregory XII and Martin V) It held 45 sessions between November 1415 and April 1418 attended by some 200 bishops* and theologians*. The council met to try to end the 'Great Schism*' (rival papacies based in Avignon and Rome, supported by different European kings).

Florence (Pope Eugenius IV) Met in Basel, Ferrara and Florence between 1431 and 1445, attended by both Latin and Greek (Catholic*, Byzantine* and other) bishops* to try and reunite the Eastern and Western Churches*. It also denied claims that an ecumenical council* is superior to the Pope*.

Lateran 5 (Popes Julius II and Leo X) Held between May 1512 and March 1517. It stated the relationship of popes* and ecumenical councils* and laid down the doctrine of indulgences*.

Trent (Popes Paul III, Julius III, Pius IV) It held 25 sessions between December 1545 and December 1563 to reform the Church* in the wake of the Reformation* and to respond to the Protestant* movement. It issued decrees concerning Scripture*, Faith*, Salvation*, Sacraments*, the Mass*, Saints*, images*, Purgatory* and Indulgences*. The council ordered a reform of the liturgy*, a catechism*, seminaries for training priests*, religious* education and many other doctrinal* and practical reforms.

Vatican 1 (Pope Pius IX) Held in Saint Peter's Basilica* between 8 December 1869 and 1 September 1870, this Council defined the dogma of papal* infallibility* and issued statements covering revelation*, faith* and reason in a dogmatic* constitution on the Catholic* faith.

Vatican 2 (Popes John XXIII and Paul VI) Announced in 1959 by John XXIII, the council first met in Saint Peter's Basilica* from 11 October to 8 December 1962. Following the Pope's* death (3 June 1963) Pope Paul VI reconvened the council for three further sessions: 29 September–4 December 1963, 14 September–21 November 1964 and 14 September–8 December 1965. The total number of bishops* participating was 2860, but average attendance was between 2000 and 2500, and 274 bishops were prevented from attending, most for political reasons.

Sixteen major documents emanated from the council, two dogmatic* and two pastoral* constitutions, nine decrees and three declarations. These were all concerned with renewal in the Church*. The titles, dates and (where appropriate) content are as follows.

Inter Mirifica Decree on the Instruments of Social Communication, 4 December 1963. The council's declaration on the media.

Sacrosanctum Concilium Dogmatic Constitution on the Liturgy*, 21 November 1964. Laid down the reasons for and process of liturgical* renewal.

Lumen Gentium Dogmatic Constitution on the Church, 21 November 1964. Gave a renewed theology of the Church as the People of God.

Unitatis Redintegratio The Council Decree on Ecumenism*, 21 November 1964. This laid down how the Catholic* Church was to become involved in ecumenical action.

Orientalium Ecclesiarum The Decree on the Eastern Catholic Churches*, 21 November 1964. The council's framework for the life and work of the churches that follow Eastern rites* and are in communion* with the Holy See*.

Christus Dominus The Decree on the Pastoral Office of Bishops, 28 October 1965.

Gravissimum Educationis The Declaration on Christian* Education, 28 October 1965.

Nostra Aetate Declaration on the relationship of the Church to non-Christian religions*, 28 October 1965. Among other issues, this document attempted to bring a new spirit into the Church's relationship with the Jewish people.

Optatam Totius The Decree on the training of priests*, 28 October 1965.

Perfectae Caritatis The Decree on the renewal of religious* life, 28 October 1965.

Apostolicam Actuositatem The Decree on the Apostolate* of the Laity*, 18 November 1965.

Dei Verbum The Dogmatic Constitution on Divine Revelation*, 18 November 1965. A theology of the sources of revelation, Scripture* and tradition* in the life of the Church.

Ad Gentes Decree on the Missionary Activity of the Church, 7 December 1965.

Dignitatis Humanae Declaration on Religious Freedom, 7 December 1965.

Gaudium et Spes Pastoral Constitution on the Church in the Modern World, 7 December 1965.

Presbyterorum Ordinis Decree on the Ministry* and Life of Priests, 7 December 1965.

PART THREE

THE SANCTIFYING CHURCH

SACRAMENTS AND
OTHER SERVICES

Christ's* work of salvation* continues in the Church* through the power of the Holy Spirit* in the sacraments. The sacraments are the principal rites* celebrated by the Church. Other rites are also celebrated, such as daily prayer* and funerals*.

Sacraments

The Latin term *sacramentum* described a military oath-taking, a ritual* of initiation. The Latin-speaking Church used the word to translate the Greek *mysterion* encompassing the dying and rising of Christ, the 'mystery* of salvation*' and a Church ritual enacting that saving work of Christ in the Holy Spirit.

In the Middle Ages* the Church fixed the number of these rites at seven. They are: baptism*, confirmation*, Eucharist* (or Mass*), marriage*, ordination*, penance*, anointing* of the sick.

Baptism (Greek *baptizein* – to dip in water) is the rite* of admission into the Church*. Baptism is celebrated by pouring water* over a person who has professed faith* in God*, Christ*, the Holy Spirit* and the Church. The words used during the pouring are 'I baptise you in the name of the Father and of the Son and of the Holy Spirit.' When children are baptised, the profession of faith is made for them by their parents or sponsors* (godparents*). Bishops*, priests*, deacons* – and in emergency cases any baptised person – may baptise. There are two rites for baptism, one for infants and one for adults, known as the 'Rite for the Christian Initiation of Adults (R.C.I.A.)*'.

Confirmation (Latin *confirmatio* – a completion, reinforcement or seal) is connected to baptism*, and is understood as the giving of the seal or mark of the Holy Spirit* on the one confirmed. The minister* – bishop* or priest* – lays hands on the candidate and anoints them with Chrism*. Children are confirmed either before First Holy Communion* or during adolescence. Adults who are received in the Rite for the Christian Initiation of Adults* are confirmed at baptism.

Eucharist (Greek *eucharistia* – thanksgiving) is the regular sacramental liturgy* of the Church*. It takes the form of a celebration of the Word* of God*, followed by a 'Eucharistic Prayer'* or thanksgiving over bread* and wine* and their sharing among the people. The bread and wine become the body and blood of Christ*, and make present his sacrifice*. Bishops* and priests* preside at the Eucharist. See **Mass**.

Marriage is the lifelong commitment to each other of a man and a woman, expressed at a wedding by the making of promises and the blessing* of the Church*. It is understood (see Ephesians* 5:21–33) as the image and expression of Christ's* love for his body*, the Church. The man and woman themselves are the ministers* of this sacrament, which is 'witnessed' and blessed by a bishop*, priest* or deacon*.

Orders (from Latin *ordo*, meaning a group of people with a particular function) is the rite which sets men aside for the exercise of ministry*: of bishop*, presbyter* (priest)*, and deacon*. The bishop is the celebrant of ordination*. He lays hands on those to be ordained*. For deacons, the bishop alone imposes his hands. For presbyters, all the priests present impose hands after the bishop, for bishops, several (usually three) bishops lay on hands. The laying on of hands is followed by the Prayer* of Ordination. See the section on 'Ministry', page 113.

Penance (from Latin *paenitentia* – repentance) is the rite by which the forgiveness of sins* is given for those who repent and do penance. The rite consists of the confession* of grave sins* by the penitent* to the priest*, the giving of a 'penance' and the giving of absolution*, a declaration of God's forgiveness through the priest. The rite exists in two forms: individual and communal. A third form known as 'general absolution'* is rarely used. Bishops* and priests are the ministers* of this sacrament.

Anointing of the Sick is the rite celebrated with those who are very ill, to give them strength from Christ* to bear their illness. The bishop* or priest* is the minister* of this sacrament. It takes the form of the imposition of hands* and an anointing* with oil (usually) blessed* previously by the bishop*.

All the sacraments may be celebrated at Mass*. Some, such as ordination*, always form part of Mass. Penance* seldom takes place at Mass.

The following paragraphs describe in detail the sacraments as they are celebrated, together with a short account of their meaning. A word list is given at the end of the following section, on page 67.

Infant Baptism

Infant baptism may be celebrated at Mass* or on its own. If it is celebrated at Mass the opening rites are done at the beginning of Mass and the baptism after the Liturgy of the Word*.

Baptism begins with the parents and godparents or sponsors* presenting the child. The priest* asks them to name the child and promise that he or she will be brought up in the Catholic* faith*. They sign the child's head with the sign of the cross*.

The Liturgy of the Word now follows. After the General Intercession* the priest anoints the child on the chest with the Oil of Catechumens*. Then the priest says a prayer* of blessing* over the water* and asks the parents and godparents to make the renunciation of sin* and profession of faith. The priest then baptises the child, dipping it in the water or pouring water on its head with the 'form'* of baptism, the words: 'N. I baptise you in the name of the Father* and of the Son* and of the Holy Spirit*'. The priest anoints the child's head with Chrism* and clothes the child in a white garment. A lighted candle* is given to the parents. Then all present say the 'Our Father*' and the rite ends with a blessing. At Mass the Liturgy of the Eucharist* follows the baptism.

Adult Baptism: Rite for the Christian Initiation of Adults (R.C.I.A.)

R.C.I.A. is a process taking sometimes many years. It culminates in the baptism*, confirmation* and first Eucharist* of those initiated.

R.C.I.A. has several stages. First is the period of 'enquiry'* where adults who express interest in the Christian* faith* are encouraged to learn about Christian teaching and think about how they respond to it. Then, if they wish to be received into the Church*, they are received as a catechumen*. These are people learning in greater depth about the Church, and beginning to live under the guidance of the Gospel*. Later, if they wish to become Catholics*, they will be enrolled as 'elect'* preparing directly for the sacraments of initiation. This enrolment, known as the 'Rite of Election'*, takes place at the beginning of Lent*. During Lent the elect celebrate 'scrutinies'* which are exorcism rites* and they may receive the Gospels, and learn the creed*. Lastly, usually at the Easter Vigil*, they profess their faith and are baptised and confirmed and for the first time receive the Eucharist.

Confirmation

For those who have been baptised* when very young, confirmation is celebrated any time between the ages of seven and eighteen years. The bishop* is the usual minister* of this sacrament, though priests* may also confirm when given permission by the Bishop (and see **Adult baptism** above). Confirmation usually takes place at Mass*, after the Liturgy of the Word*. The candidates are asked to renew the baptismal promises* and the bishop prays over them. Then he lays his hands on each candidate's head and anoints* them with Chrism* using the words: 'Be sealed with the gift of the Holy Spirit*.' He exchanges the sign of peace* with each candidate. The Liturgy of the Eucharist* follows.

Confirmation is understood as a celebration of the gifts of the Holy Spirit, given in baptism and now 'confirmed' – as the gifts necessary to lead a fully Christian* life.

The Eucharist (the Mass)

This section gives first of all the outline of the Sunday* Mass, then a short explanation of its meaning.

The Mass has two main parts: the 'Liturgy of the Word'* and the 'Liturgy of the Eucharist'*.

The Mass begins with rites of introduction, which will be an opening procession*, greeting, and an act of penance*. The hymns* 'Kyrie eleison'* and

'Gloria in excelsis'* may be sung or recited. A collect* ends the introductory rites.

The Liturgy of the Word consists of a reading from the Old Testament*, followed by a responsorial psalm*. The New Testament* reading comes next, usually from one of the Letters of the Apostles*. The chant 'Alleluia'* (or a simple acclamation* in Lent*) introduces the Gospel* reading. After the Gospel reading, the homily* is given. The homily may be based on the readings. It is followed by the creed* and the Prayer of Intercession* or 'bidding prayers'*.

The Liturgy of the Eucharist is in two main parts. As a preliminary, the bread* and wine* and other gifts are presented at the altar*. The presentation rite ends with a short prayer*, the 'Prayer over the gifts.'

Then the Eucharistic Prayer* follows, a prayer of thanksgiving and consecration*. It begins with the words 'Lift up your hearts', contains the acclamations 'Holy Holy Holy'* the 'mystery* of faith*' and ends with the doxology* and 'Amen*'.

The giving of communion* begins with the 'Our Father*' and then the bread is broken and the chalice(s) prepared for communion. After communion there is the 'Prayer after communion', the blessing* and dismissal*.

In the Mass, Christ* is present as the one who died and rose from death*. As Christ in his paschal mystery* offered himself as a sacrifice* for the life of the world, the Church* celebrates the Eucharist to enter into that act of Christ. The Eucharist is the sacrifice and the 'real presence'* of Christ under the appearance of bread and wine. Christ gives himself in this way so that the Church might have the strength to follow his way of discipleship and sacrificial love.

Marriage

The Rite of Marriage may be celebrated during Mass* or apart from Mass. In both cases it takes place after the Liturgy of the Word*.

The couple are asked to state their intention to marry. Two forms* are given for this, a simple question and answer (the church* form) and a declaration based on the civil form and required for civil recognition of the marriage. Then the promises are exchanged. Again, two forms are employed. The priest* declares the couple married. The ring(s) is(are) then blessed* and put on.

The Nuptial Blessing* follows either at the end of the marriage rite or, if the rite is during Mass, after the Our Father* in the Liturgy of the Eucharist*.

The couple are the ministers* of the sacrament to each other and the promises they make are what begins the sacrament of their marriage.

Marriage is understood as a lifelong covenant* between the spouses which imitates and reflects the covenant Christ has with the Church, which is sometimes described as his 'bride'*. Christ sealed this covenant by shedding his blood in sacrifice*. To celebrate a marriage at Mass makes this point most fully, as well as expressing the unity of the couple when they receive the Lord's body and blood* jointly in Holy Communion*.

Ordination (See also Ministry*)

The Rite* of Ordination* is always celebrated during Mass*, at the end of the Liturgy of the Word*. The candidate is presented to the congregation* and is asked questions to test his suitability for ministry*. Then the Litany of Saints* is sung while the candidate lies prostrate. Then the heart of the celebration* follows: the bishop* lays his hands on the candidate's head, then says the prayer* of ordination.

For deacons*, the bishop alone lays on hands. For priests*, the bishop and all priests present lay their hands on the head of the candidate. For bishops, the bishops present lay on hands. The Ordination Prayer is recited by the bishop alone.

Other rites follow the ordination. For all orders*, the candidate is clothed with his particular vestments*. Objects that speak of his ministry are given him, a book of the Gospels* to deacons, bread* and wine* for the Eucharist* to priests and the pastoral staff* to bishops.

Then the Liturgy of the Eucharist* follows, where the newly ordained* take part. A new diocesan* bishop at his episcopal* ordination will preside at the Liturgy of the Eucharist.

Penance

The rite* exists in three forms*, individual (the usual form), communal with individual confession* and communal with no specific confession and with communal absolution*.

The first form involves the priest* greeting the penitent* and a short reading from Scripture*. The penitent confesses sins* and the priest may give advice and counsel. The priest gives a penance* to the penitent. The penitent makes an 'act of contrition'* and the priest gives absolution. A short thanksgiving follows to end the rite.

The second form involves the celebration* of the Liturgy of the Word* and a communal examination of conscience and act of penance*. Then penitents go to the priest (usually several priests gather for this service*), confess their sins and receive absolution. The service ends with a prayer* of thanksgiving and blessing*.

The third form involves the Liturgy of the Word followed by a communal examination of conscience and act of penance. Then the priest gives absolution to the congregation*.

The Sacrament of Penance carries on the work Jesus* entrusted to the apostles* of forgiving sins (John* 20:23). In the Roman Church* the priest acts in three ways, as minister* of absolution, as counsellor in giving advice and as judge – in the giving of a 'penance'.

Anointing of the Sick

The Rite* of Anointing* may be celebrated either at Mass* or outside of Mass. If celebrated at Mass it comes after the Liturgy of the Word*. If celebrated apart from Mass, it includes a liturgy* of the word. This may be preceded by the greeting, sprinkling of holy water* and Penitential Rite*.

The priest* and the sick person(s) pray together a short litany* and the priest lays his hands on the sick. He says a prayer* over the anointing oil* and anoints the sick on the forehead and palms of the hands. There is a short prayer after the anointing and the 'Our Father'*.

Jesus* sent his apostles* out to preach* and heal the sick, as he himself had done. The New Testament* recalls how the apostles used oil to anoint (Mark* 6:13) and Saint James gives the basic shape of the service* (James* 4:13–15), which is imposition of hands* and anointing. The Sacrament of Anointing is often referred to as the 'Sacrament of the Sick' and is intended to be celebrated with all who are very ill. During the medieval period it became associated with the dying (see **Last rites**) but it is now restored as a ritual* for the sick.

Other Services in the Catholic Church

Daily Prayer or the Liturgy of the Hours

From early times Christians* prayed at specific times of day: dawn and sunset; also the third, sixth and ninth hours of the Roman day. At sunset, lamps were lit and blessed*. The third, sixth and ninth hours echoed the New Testament* accounts of the Passion* of Jesus* and the descent of the Holy Spirit* at Pentecost*.

Later, the monks* added prayers* at night to this pattern. These became known as 'Vigils'*. The tradition* of seven-fold daily prayer – Lauds*, Prime*, Terce*, Sext*, None*, Vespers*, Compline* coupled with prayer at night (known as either 'Vigils'* or 'Matins'*) – emerged in the medieval period. These 'Hours' consisted of recitation of the Psalms* (all 150 psalms in a weekly cycle), readings from Scripture* and prayers. The texts were eventually organised into a book known as the 'Breviary*'.

In the sixteenth century, the Council of Trent* revised the Roman Breviary and in 1569 mandated it for the whole Church*. This in turn was revised in 1911. Clergy* were obliged to recite the whole Office* each day.

The Second Vatican Council* renamed the Office as the 'Liturgy of the Hours'. This made Lauds and Vespers – known in English as Morning Prayer* and Evening Prayer* – the principal services*. Added to these were a single 'Midday Prayer' and 'Night Prayer'* or Compline. Finally, a new service, the 'Office of Readings'*, was introduced which could be recited at any time. This contained a Scripture Lectionary* and a reading from the Fathers*. This revised Office is mandatory on all ordained* ministers* and celebrations* of it, especially Lauds and Vespers with the people, are recommended.

Other services: See the word list for Benediction, Devotions, Stations (Way) of the Cross, Novena, etc.

Funeral Liturgy: The Order of Christian Funerals

The Catholic* funeral rites are celebrated in stages. First, there is prayer* at the time of death* and afterwards, in the home of the deceased*. This prayer is sometimes known as a 'wake'* (or vigil*) service*. Second, there is the procession* of the body and mourners to the church*, where further prayer may be celebrated, particularly if the body is brought to lie overnight in the church. Third, there is the Funeral Mass* or service. The Funeral Mass contains the 'final commendation'* where the body is sprinkled with holy water* and incense*. The last stage is to take the body to its resting place in the cemetery or to its cremation* at the crematorium where short prayers are said. Ashes may be buried.

It is customary to remember the dead on the 'Month's Mind'* one month after death, and the anniversary of death (Year's Mind*). Many parishes* have commemorations of their dead during the month of November, particularly around 1 November, All Saints' Day, and 2 November, which is the commemoration day of all the dead. Some parishes go to say prayers at their local cemetery on 2 November, and also on Holy Saturday*.

THE CHURCH'S YEAR

The Calendar: the Seasons

Sunday is the primary Christian* festival. It is the day of Christ's* Resurrection*, The 'Lord's* Day'. Sundays form the 'skeleton' of the whole Church* Year.

The Church Year is divided into seasons* that revolve round the two feasts* of Easter* and Christmas*. The Year begins with the Sundays of Advent* which lead up to Christmas and Epiphany*. The Sundays of Lent* lead up to Easter and after Easter there is a seven-Sunday, fifty-day, Easter season, which contains Ascension* Day and concludes with Pentecost*.

In addition to these is 'Ordinary Time'*, thirty-four weeks in all, which runs from Epiphany to Lent and from Pentecost to Advent. Ordinary Time will vary in length between Epiphany and Lent and Pentecost and Advent, since Easter does not have a fixed date.

The dating of Easter is linked to the Jewish feast of Passover* since Christ died and rose again at Passover. Jews keep Passover on a fixed date, the 15th of the Jewish month Nisan. Christians* came to celebrate Easter on the Sunday after the Passover. In our calendar, this date can be anywhere between 22 March and 25 April. The Second Vatican Council*, however, stated that the Catholic* Church had no objections to fixing the date of Easter.

Alongside the seasons, there are many holy days*, commemorations of events in the mission* of Christ, celebrations* of Our Lady* and the saints*. These fall on fixed dates during the year.

The seasons and holy days are marked by special liturgical* texts and ceremonies, and by liturgical colours* for vestments* and hangings.

Feasts are graded into Solemnities*, Feasts and Memorials* according to their importance.

Within the Church's Year there are also days when fasting and abstinence* are prescribed. These are Ash Wednesday* and Good Friday*. Bishops* determine other fasting days too.

The Christmas Cycle

Sundays of Advent – 1st, 2nd, 3rd, 4th. Colour*: Purple (Rose on the 3rd Sunday*)

Advent (Latin *advenire* – to come close) celebrates two 'comings' of Christ*. It begins with his coming at the end of time to judge* the world, then turns to the events and people who prepared the way for his human birth. The third Sunday* is known as *Gaudete Sunday* – from the Latin of the Introit* chant 'Rejoice' (Philippians* 4:4). The last week of Advent is a time of special preparation for Christmas*.

Christmas Day – Solemnity* – 25 December. Seasonal colour*: White or Gold.

Christmas (from 'Christ-Mass' – the Mass* of the birth of Christ*. The common 'Xmas' derives from the use of the Greek letter X [chi] which is the first two letters of the name 'Christ'). The actual date of Christ's birth is not known. The Roman *Philocalian Calendar* (336CE) is the first to mention the celebration* of Christ's birth on the December date, possibly in reaction to a pagan* feast* of the 'Birth of the Unconquered Sun' (*Dies Natalis Solis Invicti*), a midwinter solstice feast. Three masses are said, the first at night, a second at dawn and a third in the daytime.

Sundays and feasts between Christmas and Epiphany If Christmas* falls on Wednesday, Thursday, Friday or Saturday, two Sundays* will follow Christmas. The first Sunday is the Solemnity* of the Holy* Family, instituted in 1921 and moved to the Sunday after Christmas in the Roman Missal* of 1969. Also in the 1969 Missal (restoring an ancient Roman tradition) New Year's Day is kept as the Solemnity of Mary*, Mother of God*.

Epiphany – Solemnity – 6 January. Colour*: White or Gold. In Greek, *epiphaneia* means a royal visit, or revelation*. Epiphany is the celebration* of Christ*, revealed* as the Universal Saviour*. In the Roman Rite it commemorates Saint Matthew's* account of the coming of the Magi* or Wise Men to the infant Jesus* and their gifts of gold (revealing him as King) incense* (showing him as God*) and myrrh (a herb used in embalming the dead, telling of his death*). Epiphany also refers to the baptism* of Christ* and the sign* of Christ turning water* into wine* at Cana. In the Eastern* Rites Epiphany celebrates Christ's baptism. The Sunday* after Epiphany (or Monday, if Epiphany falls on a Sunday) is the Feast* of the Baptism of Christ.

The Easter Cycle

The Season of Lent Seasonal colour*: Purple. 'Lent' in Old German means 'Spring'. It is a six-week season* of preparation for Easter*. It begins on Ash Wednesday*, when ashes made from burning last year's Palm Sunday* greenery are put on the heads of congregants at Mass* as a sign of repentance* and embracing the teaching of the gospel*. During Lent, the acclamation* 'Alleluia'* is not said.

Sundays of Lent The Sundays* of Lent are identified above all by the Scripture* readings chosen for them in the Lectionary*.

The Gospel* for the first Sunday is that of the Temptation* of Christ* in the desert. This marks Lent as a season* of 'Christian* warfare' against evil. The second Sunday commemorates the Transfiguration* of Jesus*, a sign* given to strengthen the disciples* against the scandal of the Crucifixion*.

In the Catholic* Church*, those who are being baptised at Easter* are at the centre of the liturgy*. On the First Sunday, they are enrolled as 'the elect'*, those chosen for the Easter baptisms*. Then, on the Third, Fourth and Fifth Sundays of Lent, the Gospel readings (Lectionary Year A) are about faith* in

Christ as Son* of God*. The Third Sunday is about the Samaritan woman (John* 4:5–42), the Fourth is about the healing and faith of the man born blind (John 9:1–41) and the Fifth Sunday Gospel is the raising of Lazarus (John 11:1–45). For those to be baptised, there are special rites of purification known as 'scrutinies'* on these Sundays.

In Years B and C of the Lectionary the readings for the Third, Fourth and Fifth Sundays are about repentance* and reconciliation*. Where there are adults to be baptised at Easter, however, the readings for Year A must always be used.

All the congregation* is invited to keep Lent along with the 'elect' as a time of spiritual purification, of living the values of the gospel* and of prayer*.

The Fourth Sunday of Lent was a time for relaxing the fast*. It is known as *Laetare Sunday* from the Latin Introit* for the Sunday Mass*: 'Rejoice, Jerusalem!' (Isaiah* 66:10).

On the Fifth Sunday, all statues except those of the crucified Christ may be covered with purple cloth as a sign that Lent is moving towards Holy Week*, the celebration* of the Passion* (Latin *passio* – suffering) of Christ.

Palm Sunday of the Lord's Passion

Colour*: Red. The Mass* of Palm Sunday begins with a procession* carrying palms* and greenery, in commemoration of Christ's* triumphal entry into Jerusalem where people welcomed him by waving palm and olive branches. The Mass contains the reading of the Passion* from the Gospel of Matthew* in Year A of the Lectionary* cycle, Mark* in Year B and Luke* in Year C. With the Mass of Palm Sunday, Holy Week* begins.

Holy Week

– Monday to Thursday afternoon. Colour*: Purple. Before the liturgical* reforms of the Second Vatican Council* the Passion* was read at Mass* on Tuesday and Wednesday. On Wednesday, Thursday and Friday evening the rite known as Tenebrae* was celebrated.

Thursday

of this week is known as Holy Thursday or Maundy Thursday*. 'Maundy' comes from Latin *Mandatum novum*, 'I give you a new commandment', which is what Christ* said as he commanded the apostles* to follow his example and wash each others' feet as an act of love and service. It was also known as 'Sheer' (Anglo-Saxon for 'clean') Thursday because on this day penitents* who had kept Lent* as a time of atonement* for serious sins* were publicly absolved of their sins in church.

In the morning of Holy Thursday in Catholic* cathedrals* the bishop* gathers with priests* and people of the diocese*, and blesses the holy oils* which are to be used throughout the year in baptism*, confirmation* and other sacraments*. The oil for the Sacrament of Anointing* the Sick is usually blessed* during the Eucharistic Prayer* and the Oil for Baptism and the Oil of Chrism* (a mixture of olive oil and perfume) after Communion*. At this Mass the priests renew their priestly commitment.

The Sacred Triduum of the Passion and Resurrection of the Lord

Colour*: White for the Evening Mass*, Red for Good Friday* and White or Gold for Easter*.

'Triduum' in Latin means a period of three days. Between the evenings of Holy Thursday* and of Easter Sunday*, the Church's* liturgy* celebrates the dying and rising of Christ* in three 'movements'.

On **Holy Thursday** evening the Mass of the Lord's Supper* commemorates

Christ's institution* of the Eucharist*. The Gospel* at the Mass is the account of Jesus* washing his disciples'* feet (John* 13:1–15). The priest* washes the feet of twelve men from the parish* to act out this Gospel. After Mass the Blessed Sacrament* is solemnly laid up in a special chapel, to be used on Good Friday. A vigil* may be kept at the place of reservation*.

Good Friday gets its name as a corruption of 'God's* Friday'. On Good Friday, in the afternoon, the liturgy celebrates the death* of Christ. The Passion* according to John* is read, and after intercession* prayers*, a large wooden cross* is placed in the sanctuary* and venerated. Holy Communion*, set aside the previous evening, is given.

Good Friday is a popular day for the Way of the Cross* and for ecumenical* processions of witness.

On **Holy Saturday** there are no services* usually until the evening. The Easter Vigil* should begin after dusk.

The **Easter Vigil** consists of four parts. First, the 'New Fire'* and Easter Candle* are lit and blessed*. Next there are readings from the Scriptures* celebrating God's power in creation and salvation*, and the proclamation of the Easter Gospel. Third, those adults who have been preparing for baptism* and reception into the Church are baptised. The liturgy ends with the Eucharist* of Easter.

Easter Sunday and Eastertime Seasonal colour*: White or Gold. From Easter Sunday until Pentecost*, the Easter Season* lasts fifty days. Easter Sunday is reckoned as the 'First Sunday of Easter' and the Sundays* are numbered accordingly.

Easter Sunday is the day of the Lord's* Resurrection* and appearances to his disciples*. It is the greatest of all Christian feasts*. Christ* rose on the 'third day' (Good Friday* being counted as the first day), or the 'first day of the week' (in Jewish calculation the day after the Sabbath* or Saturday), or by some ancient writers on the 'Eighth Day', i.e., the eternal* day that, unlike the other seven, would have no ending.

The Ascension of the Lord Colour*: White or Gold. The Ascension is celebrated in the sixth week of Easter* on the Thursday (in some places the celebration* is moved to the following Sunday). It is a celebration of the Risen Christ* in the glory of the Father*. The New Testament* sees this as an upward movement of Christ into the heavens*, which gives the celebration its name.

Pentecost Colour*: Red. The name 'Pentecost' is Greek for 'the fiftieth day', that is, the last day of the Easter* festival. It is celebrated as the day of the descent of the Holy Spirit* on the apostles* (Acts* 2:1ff.). In English it is known also as 'Whit Sunday', perhaps because in northern Europe Easter baptisms* were sometimes deferred to this day for the sake of warmer weather and the baptised wore white robes. An alternative derivation is that the apostles received 'wit' or wisdom, from the Holy Spirit.

The Cycle of Ordinary Time

Sundays and Weekdays of Ordinary Time Seasonal colour*: Green. The thirty-four Sundays* and weeks that comprise Ordinary Time are the period between Epiphany* and Lent* and Pentecost* and Advent*. Until 1969 these Sundays were styled 'Sundays after Epiphany' and 'Sundays after Pentecost'. 'Ordinary' means, not 'common', but something like a 'series' (Latin *Ordo*) of Sundays.

The following important feasts* are kept during Ordinary Time.

Feast of the Baptism of the Lord – Sunday* after Epiphany* – First Sunday of Ordinary Time. Colour*: White or Gold. Drawing from the Eastern* tradition* of Epiphany as the Lord's* baptism*, this feast* was instituted in 1960. It celebrates the revelation* of Christ,* the Anointed One*, God's* beloved Son*.

Solemnity of Christ the King – last Sunday* of Ordinary Time. Colour*: White or Gold. This solemnity* was instituted in 1925 by Pius XI. In 1969 it was placed on the last Sunday of Ordinary Time. It celebrates Christ's* return in glory, the Last Judgement* and God's* final sovereignty over all creation.

Solemnity of the Holy Trinity – Sunday* after Pentecost*. Colour*: White or Gold. A feast* in honour of the whole event of salvation*, the work of the Father*, Son* and Holy Spirit*. It spread in the Latin Church* from monasteries* in the ninth century to the whole Church in the fourteenth century.

Solemnity of the Body and Blood of Christ – Thursday after Trinity Sunday*. Colour*: White or Gold. This feast* was formerly known as 'Corpus Christi' (Latin for 'The Body of Christ'). It arose in the thirteenth century as a celebration* of 'Transubstantiation'* or the real presence* of Christ* in the Eucharist*. It was extended to the whole Church* by Pope* Urban IV in 1264. After Mass* on this day the Blessed Sacrament* is carried in procession*.

Solemnity of the Sacred Heart of Jesus – Friday following the Sunday* after Trinity. Colour*: White. The cult of the Sacred Heart of Jesus* dates back to the Middle Ages but was only established for the whole Latin Church* in 1856 by Pope* Pius IX. It celebrates the great love of Christ* by focusing on the image* of his heart, the source and centre of God's* love for all people.

Other Holy Days

Other major holy days not mentioned in the text above are as follows.

Feast of the Presentation of the Lord Known as Candlemas, the feast* [Old English *mass*] of candles – 2 February. Colour*: White. This is the celebration* of the day when Mary* and Joseph went to the Temple to present the infant Christ* to God* (Luke* 2:22–40). Candles are blessed* and carried in procession* before Mass* on this day.

Solemnity of the Annunciation of the Lord – 25 March. Colour*: White. This feast* celebrates the coming of the Angel* Gabriel to Mary* to tell her that she was to bear Jesus* (Luke* 1:26–38). It is observed exactly nine months before Christmas*.

Solemnity of All Saints – 1 November. Colour*: White or Gold. Originally a celebration* of all martyrs*, this feast* became established in the Church* in the early Middle Ages. The liturgy* celebrates the 'New and Heavenly Jerusalem', the true home of all Christ's* holy* people.

Solemnity of Dedication of the Church – anniversary of Dedication. Colour*: White or Gold. This is celebrated in each church* on the anniversary of its dedication*.

Days of Special Prayer

Before 1969, certain days of the year were days of fasting and prayer*, known as 'ember'* days and 'rogation'* days. These were abolished in the reformed Roman Missal* of 1969.

Each conference* of bishops* in the Catholic* world may set aside certain days for special prayer intentions. In England and Wales, these days are:

World Peace (1 January); Christian Unity* (Friday between 18 and 25 January); Needy and Hungry of the World (Friday of the first week of Lent* and Friday before first Sunday* of October); Human Work (1 May or Monday before Ascension* Day); Vocations* to Priesthood* and Religious* Life (4th Sunday of Easter* or Friday before 4th Sunday of Easter); Thanksgiving for Harvest (Friday between 22 and 28 September, or nearest Sunday).

The Sunday nearest to 11 November is kept as **Remembrance Sunday**, which is a national observance. Mass* may be celebrated for those who died in war.

Word List for 'Sacraments and Other Services' and 'The Church's Year'

Ablutions (Latin *abluo* – to wash) The cleansing of the chalice* by the priest*, deacon* or minister,* which may be done either after communion* or after Mass* is over.

Absolution (Latin *absolutio* – release) The prayer* said by the priest* in the Sacrament of Penance* which declares the penitent* forgiven.

Act of contrition A prayer* said by a penitent* in the confessional* expressing sorrow for sins*.

Affusion (Latin *affundere*, to pour upon) The pouring of water in baptism* over the candidate to be baptised.

Altar (Latin *altare* – a place for burning a sacrifice*) The table on which the bread* and wine* of the Eucharist* are offered and consecrated. The altar is usually of stone and fixed. Each church* must have a fixed, dedicated altar. (See also 'The Church Building and Its Contents', page 83.)

Altar cloth(s) The covering of the table of the altar*, usually of linen. There should be at least one such cloth, though traditionally there are three, one of which reaches to the floor on the sides of the altar. The term is also used of the frontal* or coloured pall* that covers the whole altar.

Anamnesis (Greek for 'act of remembrance') The word used by Jesus* in the narrative of the Lord's Supper* in the New Testament* (Luke* 22:19, 1 Corinthians* 11:24, etc.: 'Do this in remembrance [for the anamnesis] of me.' It usually describes that part of the Eucharistic Prayer* after the narrative of the Last Supper* where the death* and Resurrection* of Christ* is commemorated. In fact the whole Eucharistic Prayer has the character of *anamnesis*.

Anaphora (Greek *anapherein* – to lift up) A name given to the Eucharistic Prayer* in the Mass*.

Anointing (Latin *unction* – anointing) The act of touching a person with oil* or pouring oil over them. In the Letter of Saint James* (4:14–17) it is commended as a ritual* for healing* and forgiveness of sins*. This is the origin of the Sacrament of Anointing* or Sacrament of the Sick*. Anointings are also part of the Rite* of Ordination* of priests* and bishops*, of the dedication* of a church*, and of the rites of Christian initiation – baptism* and confirmation.*

Asperges (Latin *aspergere* – to sprinkle) The ceremony of sprinkling the congregation* at the beginning of Sunday* Mass*, which is one of the options in the Missal* for the Penitential Rite*.

Baptismal candle The lighted candle given to the parents and sponsors*, or godparents of the baptised. It symbolises the light of faith* given through baptism*.

Baptismal garment A white garment, tunic or shawl, put on by the newly baptised, indicating that they have 'clothed themselves in Christ*'.

Baptismal promises The renouncing of evil and the profession of faith* by either the one to be baptised or their parents and sponsors*. These promises are renewed by the whole congregation* every year at the Easter Vigil*.

Baptismal sponsor Church* law is that at least one of those who present a child or adult for baptism* must be Catholics*. Their role is to help the parents bring up the child in the Catholic faith*. In the case of adult baptism*, they act as mentors to the new Catholic.

Baptismal water The water* used in baptism* is specially blessed*. At the Easter Vigil* water is blessed for baptisms in Eastertime*. At other times the blessing* is given at each baptism.

Baptism of blood According to Church* teaching, an unbaptised* person who suffers martyrdom* is said to have been baptised in their own blood.

Baptism of desire According to Church* teaching, the desire to be baptised and the faith* which inspires it are sufficient for salvation* if someone dies unbaptised*.

Benediction of the Blessed Sacrament (Latin *benedicere* – to bless) The act of blessing* with the consecrated host* displayed in a monstrance*, usually as the conclusion of a period of eucharistic exposition* or a procession*.

Bidding prayers A name for the intercession* at Mass* or other services*. The congregation* are asked or 'bidden' to pray, and fulfil their prayer* with a response* such as 'Lord*, hear our prayer.' See **General intercessions**

Blessed Sacrament A title for the celebration* of the Eucharist*, also applied more generally to the consecrated host* and chalice* given in communion* or reserved for the sick. See also **Eucharist**, **Transubstantiation**

Blessing In the Mass*, the final prayer* of the priest* before the dismissal*. It may be a simple sentence – 'May Almighty God* bless you, the Father*, the Son* and the Holy Spirit* – or it may be a 'solemn blessing' – a more complex prayer.

Both kinds, communion The practice, commended by the Second Vatican Council* as being in closer conformity to the command of Jesus* ('Drink this, all of you') of giving communion* from the chalice* as well as the host* at

Mass*. Conferences of bishops* may permit it in their territories after suitable preparation.

Bowing The act of reverence made by bending either the head or the whole body. Bowing the head at the name of Jesus* is traditional, and a deep bow is made before the altar* when the Blessed Sacrament* is not reserved on it.

Bread: for the Eucharist In the Latin Catholic* tradition*, the bread of the Eucharist* is made without yeast, simply of flour, water* and a little oil*. All Christians*, including the Latin-speaking Church*, probably used ordinary leavened bread until about the eighth century. The churches of Western Europe (and also one or two Eastern* churches under Roman influence) changed gradually to unleavened bread. This may have arisen out of desire to imitate the Last Supper*, which the Synoptic Gospels* say was a Passover* meal using unleavened bread. The Orthodox* churches have maintained the use of leavened bread for the Eucharist*.

Burse (Latin *bursa* – bag) A stiffened pouch, traditionally used to hold the folded corporal* and of the liturgical colour* of the day. See also **Chalice veil**

Canon of the Mass (Greek *kanon* – rule or norm) That part of the Eucharistic Prayer* that follows the *Sanctus* or 'Holy Holy Holy'. It was so called because, unlike the Preface*, it varied little from day to day. Since 1969 the Church* has employed several newly composed 'canons'.

Catechumen (Greek *katechoumenos* – one under instruction) In the Rite for the Christian Initiation of Adults*, one who is preparing for baptism*. Catechumens are treated in many ways as Catholics* even before baptism, having the right to a Catholic funeral* in the event of death*.

Catechumenate (Greek *katechoumenos* – one under instruction) In the Rite for the Christian Initiation of Adults*, the body of catechumens*, a recognised group within the Church*.

Celebrant (Latin *celebrare* – to celebrate) The celebrant of all Christian* liturgy* is firstly the assembled congregation*, though the term is also correctly used of the minister* – the bishop* or priest* at the Mass* – who presides at the celebration*.

Celebration (Latin *celebrare* – to celebrate) The common name given to any liturgical* or other worship* service.

Censer (Latin *incensum* – something burnt) The vessel in which incense* is burned over charcoal. The censer may be portable, hung on chains and swung, or it may be a standing censer. See also **Thurible**

Ceremonial The ritual actions and 'choreography' of liturgy*.

Ceremonial of Bishops The book that describes the rituals* specifically associated with the bishop*.

Chalice (Latin *calix* – cup) The cup which contains the wine* consecrated at Mass*. It should be made of precious or noble metal, though other fine and watertight materials are used too, such as crystal.

Chalice veil The cloth which may cover the chalice* and paten* before they are brought to the altar* at Mass*. It may be white, or of the liturgical colour* of the day.

Chrism (Greek *chrismos* – anointing oil) The mixture of oil* (traditionally olive oil) and balsam or perfume which is used in certain anointing* rites, such as those at baptism*, confirmation*, ordination* and the dedication of a church*. It should have a strong, pungent and attractive aroma.

A ciborium

Christmas Eve 24 December, the day or evening before Christmas* Day. The liturgy* provides a special Mass* for this occasion.

Ciborium (Greek *kiborion* – a container – actually a lily seed-pod, cup-shaped) The canopy, supported on columns*, sheltering the altar*. Early Christian* churches* usually had an altar with ciborium, though in the Middle Ages this tended to be reduced to a suspended canopy or tester* and in the Baroque* period to disappear altogether. The term is also used to denote the vessel used to contain the consecrated bread* at Mass* and in the tabernacle*. In origin it is a chalice* fitted with a cover or lid.

Collect (Latin *collecta* – things gathered up) The name given to the opening prayer* of Mass* and the concluding prayer at the Office*. In form it consists of an address to God*, sometimes the mention of God's attributes or actions, a petition* and a conclusion 'through Christ* our Lord*' or a more elaborated form. At Mass there are three such prayers, the first before the Liturgy of the Word*, the second after the preparation of the bread* and wine* and the third after communion*.

Collection (Latin *collectio* – gathering up) The collecting of money or other items for the needy or the support of the Church* during the Mass*.

Communicant Someone who receives Holy Communion*.

Compline The last of the daily prayer* services* or Offices*, celebrated at night before retiring. See also **Night Prayer**

Concelebration A celebration* of Mass* where several priests* are present and recite parts of the Eucharistic Prayer* together. Concelebration is proper* to Mass* where the bishop* is principal celebrant* accompanied by the priests* of his diocese*. It is, however, widely used at other times, particularly in monasteries*.

Confession (Latin *confessio* – praising God* and acknowledging one's sins*) The rite of expressing sorrow for sins, usually at the beginning of Mass*. The term is also used to describe the Sacrament of Penance*.

Consecration (Latin *consecratio* – setting apart as sacred) A ritual* action or prayer*, making an object holy* and setting it apart for a ritual use. The Eucharistic Prayer* in the Mass* is a 'prayer of consecration'; the Chrism* is 'consecrated' by the bishop* in Holy Week*.

Corporal (Latin *corpus* – body) The linen cloth, unfolded on the altar* at Mass*, on which the paten* and chalice* are placed.

Creed (Latin *credo* – I believe) The profession* of Christian* faith*. See section on 'Creeds and Councils', page 49.

Cross, sign of the (Latin *crux* – cross) An act of prayer*, made by tracing the outline of the cross* from forehead to waist, then from left shoulder to right, returning the hand to the middle. Most church* services* begin with the sign of the cross.

Cruets Vessels of metal, pottery or glass to contain the wine* and water* used at Mass*.

Cult (Latin *cultus*) the proper Latin title for the worship* of God* enacted in the liturgy*.

Dedication of a church The act of setting apart a church* building for liturgical* use. This is done at a celebration* of Mass* where the bishop* presides. The church is blessed*, the altar* and walls are anointed with Chrism* and relics* sealed beneath the altar. Each year the anniversary of the dedication is kept as a solemnity* in the dedicated church. In each diocese* the cathedral* dedication anniversary is kept as a solemnity.

Devotions Short services of prayer* used at different times of the year or for different purposes. The Way of the Cross* is a devotion, as is the rosary*. There were also devotions to the Sacred Heart*, Our Lady* and the saints*.

Dismissal (Latin *missa* – a sending forth) At the end of Mass* and other liturgies*, the congregation* is formally sent out. At Mass this is often explained by the words: 'Go in peace to love and serve the Lord*.'

Divine Office An English (UK) title for the Liturgy of the Hours*.

Elect (Latin *eligere* – to choose) In the Rite for the Christian Initiation of Adults* the 'elect' are those catechumens* enrolled at the beginning of Lent* and preparing for baptism*, confirmation* and Eucharist* at Easter*.

Elements (Latin *elementum* – part) Usually, the bread* and wine* used at Mass*.

Elevation (Latin *elevare* – to lift up) At Mass*, at the end of the Eucharistic Prayer*, the priest* holds up the paten* and chalice* during the doxology* and final 'amen'* as a gesture of offering. In the Middle Ages* it became customary for the priest also to hold up the host* after the words of institution* for the people to venerate. In the sixteenth century this practice came to include the elevation also of the chalice.

Enquiry In the Rite for the Christian Initiation of Adults*, the first period of contact between an individual and the Christian* community is known as 'enquiry', where people may come and find out about the faith* and practice of the Church*.

71

THE SANCTIFYING CHURCH

Epiclesis (Greek *epi-kalein* – to invoke) A term used among Orthodox* Christians* and sometimes among Catholics*. It describes the moment in the Eucharistic Prayer* when the Holy Spirit* is invoked to make the bread* and wine* the body and blood of Christ*. In a more general sense, the whole Eucharistic Prayer has the character of *epiclesis*. See also **Invocation**

Epistle (Latin *epistola* – letter) The New Testament* reading at Mass* before the Gospel*, usually from the Letters* (Epistles*), though the term was formerly used of any first reading.

Eucharist (Greek *eucharistia* – thanksgiving) A name for the Mass*, taken from the opening words of the Eucharistic Prayer*: 'Let us give thanks to the Lord* our God*.'

Eucharistic adoration (Latin *adorare* – to pray to) The practice of sustained silent prayer* before the Blessed Sacrament*. See also **Exposition**

Eucharistic fast Before receiving Holy Communion*, those who are able to do so must fast* for at least one hour from all food and drink except water*.

Eucharistic Prayer (Greek *eucharistia* – thanksgiving) The principal prayer* of the Mass*. The General Instruction in the Roman Missal* describes it as the 'centre and high point of the celebration*'. It begins with the dialogue: 'Lift up your hearts/Let us give thanks to the Lord* our God*' and ends with the doxology*: 'Through him, with him, in him, in the unity of the Holy Spirit*, all glory and honour is yours, almighty Father*, for ever and ever.' It is a prayer of thanksgiving and consecration*.

Evening Prayer An English term for the Office* of Vespers*.

Ewer A large jug for water, of metal or ceramic, often found in churches to carry water to the font*.

Exposition (Latin *expositio* – showing) The rite* of placing the Blessed Sacrament* in a monstrance* for adoration* by the congregation*. Exposition may be perpetual, i.e. day and night, or for more limited periods. See also **Benediction** and **Eucharistic adoration**

Fast The religious* act of going without a measure of food. Formerly, the season* of Lent* was an obligatory fast, as well as certain other days. Now, the two major fast days are Ash Wednesday* and Good Friday* as well as other days which the bishops' conference* may determine. See also **Abstinence**

Feast (Latin *festum* – festival) A holy day* second in rank to a solemnity*.

Feria (Latin *feria* – holiday) A day when there is no special commemoration such as a Sunday*, saint's* day or festival.

Ferial (Latin *feria* – holiday) of or pertaining to a feria*.

Final Commendation and Farewell The concluding part of the Funeral Mass* or service, when the body of the dead person is sprinkled with Holy water* and incense*, to prepare it for burial or cremation.

Flagon With the adoption of communion in both kinds* it is necessary to provide more wine* than one chalice* will hold. The excess is often put into a flagon, to avoid multiplying chalices.

Form, sacramental (Latin *forma* – shape or likeness) The theological term used to describe the words that enact the sacraments*, as for example, the words 'I absolve you from your sins*' in the Sacrament of Penance*.

Forty Hours Devotion A period of solemn exposition* of the Blessed Sacrament* lasting about forty hours. The Forty Hours originated in the seventeenth century as a means of intensifying prayer before the Blessed Sacrament.

Fraction (Latin *fractio* – breaking) The breaking of the bread* at Mass* before communion*. The General Instruction in the Roman Missal* says that the bread should be large enough to be broken into many pieces. The fraction is accompanied by the chant* 'Agnus Dei'* (Lamb of God*).

Funeral (Latin *funereus* – of a funeral) The disposal of the body of the dead either by burial* or cremation*, with the rites* of the Church*.

General absolution (Latin *absolutio* – setting free, forgiveness) In the Sacrament of Penance* an alternative form whereby many penitents* receive absolution* all at once. It may only be used when there is too great a number of penitents for the priest* to see individually.

Genuflection (Latin *genu* – knee, and *flectere* – to bend) The gesture of bending the right knee as a sign of reverence at the consecration* at Mass* or when passing by the tabernacle* where the Blessed Sacrament* is kept.

Gospel (Old English *god spel* – good news) The accounts in the New Testament* of the life and death of Jesus*. At Mass*, the Gospel is the last of the readings in the Liturgy of the Word*.

Gradual (Latin *gradus* – step) A name for the psalm* chant* sung between the readings when Mass* is celebrated in Latin. It was originally sung from the steps of the ambo*.

High Mass Formerly, the Mass* celebrated with the greatest solemnity, usually with priest*, deacon* and subdeacon*, servers, singing and incense*. Since the revised Missal* of 1970, the ceremonial distinctions between Masses have been abolished.

Holy Communion The act of receiving the body and blood of Christ* at Mass*. Communicants* may receive the body of Christ* on the tongue or in the hand. They may also receive from the chalice* as an option. Holy Communion is given as part of the Mass, but in exceptional circumstances, such as sickness or viaticum*, it may be given from the reserved sacrament*.

Holy Order (Latin *ordo* – a group of people with a particular function) The sacrament by which ministers* are made in the Church. See also **Order**

Holy table An alternative name for the altar*.

Holy water Water* that has been blessed* (sometimes with a little salt added to keep it clean) and is used to sprinkle the people at Mass* or with which they sprinkle themselves on entering the church* See also **Asperges** and **Stoup**

Homily (Latin *homilia* – address) The homily takes place at Mass*, after the Gospel*, when the priest* or deacon* draws out the significance of the Eucharist* for that day, in the context of the readings that have been heard. A homily may also be given at the Liturgy of the Hours* and other services*.

Hosanna (Hebrew *hosha'na* – save us, we pray!) The shout of acclamation from Psalm 118:25, used by the crowds at Jesus' entry into Jerusalem on Palm Sunday* to name him as the Messiah (see **Christ**). In the liturgy*, the word occurs in the Eucharistic Prayer* at the 'Holy Holy Holy'*.

Host (Latin *hostia* – a sacrificial offering) The name given to the bread* prepared for Mass*, usually used whether this bread is consecrated or not.

Immersion (Latin *immergo* – to dip) The method of baptism* which involves the candidate being stood in water and having water poured all over the body, or even being thrust into water entirely.

Imposition of hands The ancient gesture of setting apart or consecration*. At ordination*, the bishop* (and others) lay on hands on the person to be ordained*.

In confirmation* the bishop lays hands on the candidate. In the Anointing of the Sick* the priest* lays hands on the sick person before anointing them.

Incense (Latin *incensum* – something burnt) Any one of a number of natural resins which when heated give off a sweet aroma and smoke. Incense is an ancient accompaniment to worship* and in Christian* use is burnt in a censer* or thurible*. The smell was considered an offering to God*, a symbol* of prayer* rising, and a source of purification. Frankincense, brought by the Magi* to Christ*, is one of these resins.

Institution, words of (Latin *instituere* – to set up, order or institute) The command given by Jesus* at the Last Supper* that the Church* should celebrate the Eucharist* as the body and blood of Christ*, and the defining action ('liturgy') of the Church, cf. Matthew 26:26–29, Mark 14:22–25, Luke 22:14–20, 1 Corinthians 11:23–27.

Intercession (Latin *intercedere* – to intervene, and *intercessio*) Prayers of petition* made at Mass* after the creed* or during other services* on behalf of the Church*, all humankind and for particular needs. See also **Bidding prayers**

Intinction (Latin *tingere* – to stain) One of the ways Holy Communion* may be received. The priest* dips the consecrated host* into the consecrated wine* and gives it to the communicant* on the tongue.

Introit (Latin *introire* – to enter, hence *introitus*) The psalm* chant* that accompanies the entrance procession* at Mass*.

Jesus Prayer The phrase 'Lord* Jesus* Christ*, Son* of God*, have mercy on me a sinner*' used as a form of repetitive prayer* among Orthodox* Christians* and increasingly among Catholics* and others. It is used to achieve a union of mind and heart in prayer. A prayer rope*, similar in form to the rosary*, may be used.

Last Supper According to the Synoptic Gospels*, the Passover* meal Jesus* took with his disciples* the night of his arrest and where he instituted the Eucharist*. In the Gospel of Saint John*, the Last Supper takes place before the Passover. The institution of the Eucharist is not recorded. Saint John* records that Jesus washed the feet of his disciples.

Lauds (Latin *laudes* – praises) Now usually known as Morning Prayer*, the Office* of daybreak. Traditionally, the last three psalms* of the Psalter*, which are all psalms of praise, were recited every day at Lauds. This practice was not retained in the Liturgy of the Hours*.

Lavabo (Latin *lavabo* – I shall wash (Psalm* 26:6)) In the Mass* until 1969, the words which the priest* said on washing his hands after preparing the bread* and chalice*. In the 1969 Mass, he says 'Lord*, wash me from my iniquity.'

Lavabo dish The dish used in the lavabo*.

Lavabo towel The towel used to wipe the priest's* hands in the lavabo*.

Lenten veil The veil*, usually purple in colour, that is used to cover statues and crosses* during Holy Week*.

Litany A prayer*, usually intercessory, with frequent repeated responses*, sung at solemn moments, such as ordinations*, or in procession*.

Litany of the Saints A particularly solemn form of litany*, invoking the prayers of the saints by name.

Liturgical (Greek *leitourgia* – from *laos* – the people, and *ergon* – work) Of or pertaining to the liturgy*.

Liturgical colours The colours used in vestments* and hangings in church* throughout the year. The Roman Rite* employs four principal colours: Violet

(Advent*, Lent*) White (Christmas*, Epiphany*, Easter*), Red (Pentecost* and feasts* of Martyrs*) and Green (Ordinary Time*). Rose may be used on the Third Sunday* of Advent and the Fourth Sunday of Lent*. Black may be used at funerals* and on All Souls'* Day.

Liturgy (Greek *leitourgia* – from *laos* – the people, and *ergon* – work) A word used in the Graeco-Roman world to describe a statutory duty attached to public office. Early Christians* adopted it to refer to the Mass* and other services* of the Church*. In the Orthodox* churches it is the usual title for the Eucharist*. Liturgy is sometimes referred to also as 'the work of God'.

Liturgy of the Eucharist In the Mass*, the name given to the Eucharistic Prayer* and communion*.

Liturgy of the Hours (Latin *Liturgia Horarum*) The proper title for the services* that constitute the daily prayer* of the Church*.

Liturgy of the Word In the Mass*, the name given to the first part of the service*, including the readings, homily* and intercessions*.

Lord's Prayer The prayer* taught by Christ* to the disciples* in Matthew* 6:9–13 (cf. Luke* 11:2–5), possibly based on a Jewish original known as the *Kaddish*. It is regarded as the model of all prayer and is recited at all liturgies*. At Mass* it forms the principal prayer in preparation for Holy Communion*.

Lord's Supper Saint Paul's* name (See 1 Corinthians* 11:20) for the Eucharist*.

Low Mass Formerly a celebration of Mass* without music or ministers*. See **High Mass**

Mass (Latin *missa* – dismissal) The usual name for the celebration* of the Eucharist*. It comes from the words of the dismissal* in Latin: *Ite, missa est* – 'Go, this is the dismissal.'

Mass, Canon of the (Latin *canon missae*) Now known as the First Eucharistic Prayer*, it is the ancient Roman form of that portion of the Eucharistic Prayer* that follows the Sanctus*.

Mass, Common/Ordinary of (Latin *ordinarius* – normal) Those parts of the Mass* that do not change from day to day.

Mass, order of The shape or plan of the celebration* of the Eucharist*.

Mass, Proper of (Latin *proprium* – belonging to) Those parts of the Mass* that change according to the season*.

Matins An alternative name for the Office* of Vigils* or Night Office (now known as the Office of Readings*), to distinguish it from Lauds*, to which it is often attached in monasteries*.

Memorial (Latin *memoria* – commemoration) The lowest rank of saint's* day. The keeping of memorials may either be obligatory or optional.

Midday Prayer In the post Second Vatican Council* Divine Office*, instead of the former four 'little hours' of Prime*, Terce*, Sext* and None* one single service* was proposed for the middle part of the day. This is known popularly as Midday Prayer.

Missal (Latin *missale* – mass-book) In the Roman Rite* before 1969, the Missal was the book that contained all the texts for Mass* throughout the year. See section on 'Liturgical Books'. Since 1969, the Missal is properly the term used to describe the whole range of texts for Mass, which are contained in two books, the Missal and the Lectionary*.

Monstrance (Latin *monstrare* – to display) A vessel of late medieval origin, based on a reliquary*, designed in the form of a small shrine*, or rayed circle, containing a glass window, to display the Blessed Sacrament* for adoration* or to carry it in procession*.

Month's Mind The celebration* of Mass* one month after someone's death*, as a commemoration.

Morning Prayer The English name for the Office* of Lauds*.

Moveable feast Some holy days*, e.g. Easter*, Ascension* and Pentecost*, do not fall on a fixed date, but will vary in date from year to year.

New Fire The bonfire lit and blessed* at the beginning of the Easter Vigil*, from which the paschal candle* is lighted.

Night Prayer The English name for the Office* of Compline*.

None (Latin *nona* sc. *hora* – ninth hour) in the pre-Second Vatican Council* Breviary*, the short Office* recited in the afternoon.

Novena (Latin *novem* – nine) A nine-days prayer*, preceding a feast*, or to a Saint*, or to obtain some favour.

Nuptial blessing (Latin *nuptialis* – concerning marriage) The solemn prayer* of blessing* spoken over the bride and groom. In a Nuptial Mass* it comes after the Our Father* in the Liturgy of the Eucharist*. When a marriage* is celebrated without a Mass, it comes at the end of the service*.

Nuptial Mass (Latin *nuptialis* – concerning marriage) The Mass* celebrated at a marriage*.

Offertory In the Tridentine Mass*, the name given to the preparation of the bread* and wine*. In the 1970 Mass, the term 'Preparation of the Gifts' is used instead. The term 'offertory' survives in the Roman Gradual* to name the chant* sung at the preparation of the gifts.

Office (Latin *Officium* – duty) A name given to the Liturgy of the Hours*. As something obligatory for the clergy*, it came to be called 'the Office'.

Office of Readings The name given in the post-Second Vatican Council* Liturgy of the Hours* to the service* that contains two lengthy readings, one from Scripture* and the other from the Fathers*. The Office of Readings is not tied to any particular hour of the day.

Oil of Catechumens The oil* used in baptism*. In the Rite for the Christian Initiation of Adults*, the catechumens* are anointed with it.

Oil of the Sick The oil* used in the Sacrament of Anointing* of the Sick.

Oils The use of oil is widespread in the Liturgy*. In baptism*, candidates are anointed with 'Oil of Catechumens'* before baptism and with Chrism* after it. In confirmation* and the ordination* of bishops* and priests*, the candidate is anointed with Chrism*. Newly dedicated churches* and altars* are also anointed with Chrism*. The sick are anointed with 'Oil of the Sick'*. These oils are blessed* and consecrated each year by the bishop and priests of the diocese*, usually on Holy Thursday*.

Ordinary of the Mass (Latin *ordinarius* – what is arranged) The parts of the Mass* that do not change according to the season*.

Pall (Latin *pallium* – a cloak) Either the large cloth that covers an altar* table and reaches to the ground on all sides, or the large white cloth laid upon the coffin at a funeral*, or the stiffened linen square that is used to cover the chalice* during the Eucharistic Prayer*.

Paten (Latin *patena* – a basin) The shallow plate that holds the bread* for the Eucharist*

Pax see **Sign of peace**

Penitent (Latin *paenitens* – one who repents) The name describing a person who goes to the Sacrament of Penance* to confess sins and receive absolution*.

Penitential Rite (Latin *paenitentia* – penance) The short rite* at the beginning of Mass* which contains a prayer* of sorrow for sins* and a short absolution*.

Prayer rope A rope with many knots, used to aid repetitive prayer* such as the Jesus Prayer*. The rosary* employs another form of this rope.

Preface (Latin *praefatio* – something spoken aloud) In the Mass*, the opening paragraphs of the Eucharistic Prayer*, containing the thanksgiving. The Preface changes with the liturgical* season*. It ends with the chanting* of the *Sanctus* or 'Holy Holy Holy'. The post-Second Vatican Council* Roman Mass has eighty-four prefaces. See **Proper Preface**

Presider The minister* who leads any liturgy*.

Prime (Latin *prima sc. hora* – the first hour) In the pre-Second Vatican Council* Breviary*, the first of the prayer* services* that took place during the day.

Procession (Latin *procedere* – to proceed) The ordered movement of a body of people from one place to another during a liturgy*.

Profession of faith The proper title of the creed. See **Creed**

Proper of the Mass (Latin *proprium* – belonging to) The parts of the Mass* that change according to the season* or feast*.

Proper Preface (Latin *proprium* – belonging to) The Eucharistic Prayer* preface* for a festival or special occasion.

Psalm prayer A short prayer* sometimes recited at the conclusion of a psalm*, based on the content of the psalm.

Purificator (Latin *purificare* – to cleanse) The linen napkin used to wipe the chalice* after each communicant* has received from it.

Pyx (Greek) The small vessel, made like a small box or locket, used to carry the Blessed Sacrament* to the sick.

Real presence The teaching of the Church* that Our Lord* Jesus* Christ* is really, truly and substantially present in the Eucharist*, that by transubstantiation*, the eucharistic* bread becomes the body of Christ* and the wine* becomes the blood of Christ.

Renunciation (Latin *renuntiare* – to reject) The promise to reject Satan and all his works, made by the candidate (or in their name) at the baptism* service.

Requiem Mass (Latin *missa* – mass, and *requiem* – rest) The Mass* celebrated at a funeral, and any Mass for the dead. The title is derived from the opening words of the Introit*: *Requiem aeternam . . .* 'Rest eternal . . .'

Reservation, Blessed Sacrament The practice of keeping some of the bread* consecrated at Mass* for communion* to the sick and as a focus for prayer*. Early Christians* took portions of the consecrated bread from the Eucharist* to bring communion to those who were sick or in prison. The Sacrament* was kept in church* buildings in the Middle Ages, usually in a hanging pyx* or wall aumbry* or freestanding shrine*, or on the altar* in what became known as a tabernacle*. This is the more usual method of reservation nowadays.

Rite (Latin *Ritus*) The order or pattern of celebrating the liturgy*, or the texts that it contains. The term is also used to describe the whole religious* culture of a particular group, such as in the name 'Christians* of the Byzantine Rite*'.

Rite of Election In the Rite for the Christian Initiation of Adults*, the service that is held at the beginning of Lent* to 'elect' or set apart those who are to receive baptism* and confirmation* and Holy Communion* at the forthcoming Easter*.

THE SANCTIFYING CHURCH

Ritual (Latin *ritualis* – the adjective from *ritus* – rite) Another term for rite*.

Roman Rite The liturgical* traditions of the Roman Church* for celebrating the Eucharist* and all other services, which have spread thoughout the Catholic Church.

Rosary The recitation of the Hail Mary* in fifteen sets of ten repetitions. Each set recalls one of the events of salvation*. There are three sets of five mysteries* each, 'Joyful' (events surrounding the Birth of Christ*), 'Sorrowful' (the Passion* of Christ)' and 'Glorious' (The Resurrection* of Christ). Originally the rosary was a devotion for monastic lay* brothers* who, being illiterate, could not recite the 150 Psalms*; 150 Hail Mary's were substituted. The devotion* was popularised by the Dominicans*, and in the sixteenth century assumed the form we have today. The term is also used of the series of small linked beads used to count the prayers*. It is basically a form of repetitive prayer such as is found in most religions*.

A rosary

Rubric (Latin *ruber* – red) A ceremonial* directive in a liturgical* book, traditionally printed in red to distinguish it from the prayer* text, printed in black, that it accompanies.

Sacrifice (Latin *sacer* – holy, and *facere* – to make or do) The term for giving something wholly to God*. The Church* interprets Jesus'* death and Resurrection* as a sacrifice and also the Eucharist* as a sacrifice, in as much as it enacts the dying and rising of Christ*.

Sacristan (Latin *sacristia* – the store for sacred vessels) The minister* who looks after the liturgical* goods of a church* and who prepares the altar* and vestments*, etc., for Mass*.

Sanctus (Latin for 'holy') The hymn* sung in the Eucharistic Prayer* after the Preface*, from Isaiah* 6:3. See **Holy Holy Holy**

Sanctus bell A bell, rung during Mass* at the Sanctus* to inform people that the consecration* is approaching, and again at the elevation* during the Eucharistic Prayer*. Bells, gongs and chimes may be used.

Sanctus candle In the Tridentine Mass*, a small candle* near the altar*, lit at the Sanctus* and extinguished after communion*, as a sign of reverence for the real presence*.

Scrutinies (Latin *scrutinium* – a look inside) In the Rite for the Christian Initiation of Adults*, the scrutinies are celebrated on the Third, Fourth and Fifth Sundays* of Lent* with those who are to be baptised at the coming Easter Vigil*. They have the character of exorcism* rituals*, which seek to discern the further need of growth in the Christian* life and to free the candidates from slavery to sin*.

Sermon (Latin *sermo* – a discourse) An address on an aspect of Church* teaching or practice, which may or may not form part of the liturgy*. The sermon is to be distinguished from a homily*, which is an integral part of the celebration* of Mass.*

Server (Latin *servire* – to serve) A man or woman who assists the priest* and deacon* at Mass*, particularly with the preparation of the altar*. See the section on 'Ministry'.

Sext (Latin *Sexta* – sc. *hora* – the sixth hour) In the pre-Second Vatican Council* Breviary*, the name given to the short prayer* service* recited about midday.

Sign of peace Before communion* at Mass*, the priest* asks all present to give each other a sign of peace. The form this takes is decided by the conference of bishops*. In most Western countries it is usually a handshake. The action may be accompanied by the words 'Peace be with you/And also with you'.

Solemnity (Latin *Solemnitas*) The highest rank of festival in the Catholic Church*, such as Easter*, Christmas* and Pentecost*. All Sundays* rank as solemnities also.

Species (Latin *species* – appearance) In medieval philosophy, the appearance of something was understood as being separate (though normally not separable) from its substance or reality. The terms were used to define how Christ* is present in the Eucharist*. The bread* and wine* of the Eucharist* are understood as possessing the appearances of bread and wine while being in reality or substantially the body* and blood of Christ.

Stations of the Cross (Latin *statio* – a halt on a march) A devotion*, based on fourteen incidents, some scriptural, some legendary, in the Passion* of Christ*. The devotion is done in procession* around the church*, stopping at fourteen places where small crosses* are hung, sometimes with a representation of the incident concerned. The 'Stations' are popular during Lent*. The devotion derives from medieval Holy Land pilgrimage* customs connected with the Franciscan* order* of stopping for prayer* along the Way of the Cross in Jerusalem*.

Tenebrae (Latin *tenebrae* – darkness) The service of Vigils* and Lauds* for Maundy (Holy) Thursday*, Good Friday* and Holy Saturday*, celebrated the evening before. The name comes from the extinguishing of the candles at intervals during the service, leaving total darkness at the end. Tenebrae was abolished after the Second Vatican Council*, but its popularity has grown in recent years, often as a vehicle for the great polyphonic music written for it.

Terce (Latin *tertia* sc. *hora* – the third hour) In the pre-Second Vatican Council* Breviary*, the short Office* recited at the third hour of the day in the morning after Prime*.

Thurible (Latin *thus* – incense) See **Censer**

Thurifer (Latin *thus* – incense) The server* who carries the thurible* and the incense* at Mass* and other services*.

Transubstantiation (Latin prefix *trans* – change, and *substantia* – essence) The way the Church* explains its faith* in the real presence* of Christ* in the Eucharist*. After the Eucharistic Prayer* of the Mass*, or consecration*, the appearances of bread* and wine* remain, but their reality is changed into the reality of Christ's* body* and blood. Transubstantiation was established as a dogma* by the Fourth Lateran Council* of 1215.

Tridentine Mass The form of Mass* made mandatory in 1570 for the Catholic* Church*

A thurible

79

by the reforms after the Council of Trent*. It was an attempt to restore the pure Roman liturgy*, but was basically the Mass as said in the Pope's* chapel* in the Middle Ages. The Tridentine Missal* went through many editions to allow new feasts* to be added. The last of these was in 1962. The Tridentine Mass was discontinued after the Second Vatican Council* and a newly reformed Missal used. Many Catholics* desired to be able to celebrate the former liturgy, and this permission was granted in 1988.

Unleavened bread The bread normally employed by the Roman Rite* at Mass*. See **Bread**

Veil (Latin *velum* – veil) A cloth covering for pictures and statues in church*. Also the covering of the chalice* and paten* at Mass*. See **Chalice veil** and **Lenten veil**)

Vespers (Latin *vesper* – evening) The name given to the evening Office* in the Liturgy of the Hours*, celebrated at the end of the working day and the coming of dusk. See **Evening Prayer**)

Viaticum (Latin *viaticum* – food for the journey) The giving of Holy Communion* to those who are close to death*, to strengthen them for their journey. Catholics* are under obligation, if possible, to receive communion* before death.

Vigil (Latin *vigilia* – night watch) A liturgy* taking place in the evening or at night. The ancient belief was that Christ* would come again at night (see **Parousia**), and communities honoured the most important festivals by keeping a vigil, with psalms* and readings from Scripture*. The most important vigil is that of Easter* (see **Easter Vigil**). Part of the service* for funerals* may be a vigil in prayer* for the dead person (see **Wake**).

Vigils (Latin *vigiliae* – night watches) The name given in monasteries* to the Office* celebrated at night or in the early hours before dawn (see **Matins**).

Wafer The bread* used at Mass* is unleavened and made only of flour and water*, baked between heated and oiled surfaces, usually stamped with a crucifix* or other symbol*. See also **Unleavened bread, Host, Bread**

Wake The name given to a vigil* service* held as part of a funeral*, usually a mixture of prayer* and socialising.

Water In the Graeco-Roman world, it was necessary to add water to wine*, which was often sold in a concentrated form in order to prevent it becoming sour or mouldy. This usage passed into Christian* liturgy*, with the mixing of a small quantity of water into the eucharistic wine* in the chalice*. It was subsequently understood allegorically as representing the union of human (water) and divine (wine) natures in Christ*, or as the blood and water that came from his side on the cross*. See **Baptismal water, Holy water**

Way of the Cross See **Stations of the Cross**

Wine The fermented juice of the grape used by Jesus* at the Last Supper* and so in the celebration of Mass*. Until the end of the medieval period in the Roman Rite* (and still among Orthodox* Christians*) the use of red wine at the Eucharist* was the more common, but more recently white wine has come to be used. Since the nineteenth century, it has been common in Northern Europe and the USA to use wine fortified with grape alcohol to help storage.

THE CHURCH BUILDING AND ITS CONTENTS

Church Architecture (from Greek *archos* – a master, and *tekton* – a builder)

Most Catholic* churches* were built in the nineteenth or twentieth century and reflect the architecture of the time.

In the nineteenth century the revived Gothic style* was popular for churches. In an attempt to recreate the Middle Ages, which were regarded as the 'Age of Faith*', architects designed churches in the style of the thirteenth and fourteenth centuries. Revival Gothic is characterised by high buildings, slender columns*, pointed arches, large windows, tall towers, spires* and elaborate decoration. The Gothic Revival* was associated with a revival also in traditional craftsmanship for the furnishing of churches: stained glass*, tiles, woodwork, fabrics and metalwork.

Gothic Revival: St Chad's, Birmingham

Other ancient styles were also 'revived' or imitated. The Romanesque style* was used, as was the Byzantine style*. These were characterised by rounded arches, massive piers* and small windows. Decoration was often applied in marble and mosaic, or painting. These two styles were used because they were very adaptable to the Roman liturgy*. Nineteenth-century Catholic worship* demanded a wide space, uninterrupted by columns, for everyone to see the altar*.

81

Byzantine: Westminster Cathedral, London

The classical* styles were also employed, in imitation of the great Baroque* churches of Europe, from which many Catholics* originated. These styles were characterised by use of the dome* and the classical orders* to create wide spaces and prominent altars. Elaborate decoration was often employed, intended to appeal to the emotions and people's sense of the dramatic.

Examples of these imitative styles are the Catholic cathedrals* in New York (USA) and in Birmingham (UK) in the Gothic Revival style. Westminster Cathedral in London and the National Shrine* of the Immaculate Conception*, Washington DC (USA) are in the Romanesque/Byzantine style. The Cathedral of Seattle (USA) and the Brompton Oratory* in London are classical buildings.

Classical: Brompton Oratory, London

After the First World War, Modernism produced stark and undecorated interiors, while the Liturgical Movement* with its emphasis on people offering the Mass* with the priest* required an altar that was closer to the congregation*. The best-known examples of modern styles are the Catholic Cathedral of Christ* the King

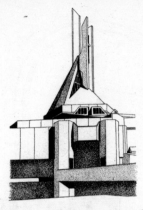

Modernist: Liverpool Roman Catholic Cathedral

in Liverpool (UK) which has the altar in the middle of a great circular space and Saint Mary's* Cathedral, San Francisco (USA).

Word List

Abacus (Latin for 'slate' or 'board') The top of a capital*, like a cushion between capital and architrave*.

Abutment (Old French *aboutement* – a support or junction) A masonry wall, pier* or buttress* which sustains the thrust of an arch or vault.

Aisle (Latin *ala* – wing, French *aile*) A corridor flanking the main nave* of a church*, divided from it by an arcade* or row of columns*. Sometimes used to describe the main walkway up the centre of the nave.

Altar (Latin *ara* or *altare* – a place of sacrificial burning) The place where the Eucharist* is celebrated. The altar is of stone or other durable material and takes the form of a table or block. The top surface or slab is known as the *mensa** (Latin – table). A dedicated church* must have a fixed altar. Relics* of saints* may be sealed into the pedestal underneath the *mensa*. The term is also used to define the sanctuary*, or the whole area around the altar table.

Altar pall See **Pall**

Altarpiece Ornamental panels, paintings or sculpture, standing on or behind an altar*.

Altar rails In early and medieval churches* the altar* area was divided from the nave* by a screen of stone or wood. In the Baroque* period this became a low rail where people knelt for communion*.

Altar of repose The place where the Blessed Sacrament* is kept after the Mass* of Holy Thursday* for use on Good Friday*. It is often used as a place for prayer* and keeping watch.

Ambo (From the Greek *anabainein* – to ascend) The raised platform where the Scripture* readings are spoken at the liturgy*. Churches* should have a fixed ambo to reflect the dignity of the Word* of God*. The ambo is used for the readings and the homily*.

The interior of a Roman Catholic church

Ambulatory (Latin *ambulare* – to walk) A continuous passageway round a building. In churches* the ambulatory was used to allow processions* and pilgrimages* to circulate.

Angelus bell The church* bell used to indicate the time for saying the Angelus*.

Antependium (Latin *ante* – in front of, and *pendere* – to hang) A hanging or ornamental cover for an altar*, made of metal, panelling or rich fabric, also known as a frontal*.

Apse (Greek *aptein* – to enclose or hold) The semicircular (or 'apsidal') sanctuary* of some churches*. In early medieval churches there was often an apse at both ends of the building. In England, the sanctuary was square rather than semicircular.

Arcade (Latin *arcus* – arch or bow) A row of open or closed ('blind') arches supported on piers* or columns*.

Architrave (Latin *arcus* – arch, and *trabs* – beam) The horizontal beam which is supported by a series of columns*.

Arris (Latin *arista* – a spine) The vertical edge between the flutes* of a column*, or the sharp edge of a brick.

Ashlar Cut stones used in building to supply a facing for a wall.

Aspergillum (Latin *aspergere* – to sprinkle) A bunch of greenery (or a metal or wooden brush) used to sprinkle holy water*.

Aumbry (Latin *armarium* – chest or cupboard) A cupboard, usually recessed into a wall, used to store sacred vessels, the holy* oils* or, in medieval churches*, the Blessed Sacrament*.

Baldacchino (medieval English *bawdekyn* – a rich and heavy silk fabric) A canopy, originally of cloth, made to be held over a sacred object. The term is used to describe the ciborium* or canopy supported on columns* which shelters the altar* in some churches*.

Banner A decorated cloth panel carried in processions*, usually as the emblem of a church*, guild or sodality*.

Baptismal font (Latin *fons* – spring) A common way of referring to the place of baptism* in a church*.

Baptismal shell A scallop-shaped container sometimes used to pour water* at baptism*.

Baptistery (Greek *baptizein* – to dip or wash) The place in a church* where baptism* is celebrated. This may be a separate room, or part of the body of the church.

Baroque A style of architecture originating in the sixteenth century, based on the architecture of ancient Rome and Greece, and characterised by grandeur of scale, large arched and domed spaces and elaborate design.

Barrel vault A tunnel-like, semicircular, continuous vault.

Basilica (Greek *Basileus* – a king) A large public hall used by the Greeks and Romans, with a semicircular apse* at one or both ends. Early Christians* adapted the basilica for liturgical* use. Nowadays, the Holy See* gives the title to church* buildings of particular significance, such as major pilgrimage* sites.

Bay (French *baie* – recess or niche) The division of a large building which may be marked by columns*, piers* or other architectural means.

Beam, collar In a wooden roof, the horizontal beam inserted across the space between two opposed sloping rafters, forming the lower edge of a triangle, to stiffen the roof.

Beam, hammer A curtailed beam projecting from the foot of a rafter, often used as a support for a curved beam above.

Beam, tie A beam that ties together the bases of two opposite rafters, spanning the roof space.

Belfry A tower* or structure containing bells, attached to the church* or standing separately. The term is also used for the space in the tower where the bells are hung.

Bell tower Another term for **Belfry**.

Bier A frame, stretcher or trolley for carrying a coffin to burial*. The term is also used to describe a catafalque*.

Boss A carved or painted block of stone or wood, placed at the intersection of ceiling ribs* in a vault*.

Brass A memorial tablet* with figures or inscription, usually found on the walls of a church* or in the floor. A popular pastime is 'brass rubbing' where the impression of the brass is imprinted on a sheet of heavy paper placed over the brass and rubbed with dark wax.

Bugia A small hand-held candleholder, once used at pontifical* Mass*.

Buttress (French *bouter* – to lean against) A brick or masonry support, built against a wall to hold it up. See also **Flying buttress**

Byzantine A style of building emphasising round arches and vaulted or domed spaces with much emphasis on marble and mosaic.

Campanile (Latin *campana* – a bell) A bell tower* usually standing apart from the church*.

THE SANCTIFYING CHURCH

Candlesnuffer A device for putting out tall candles*, usually in the form of a hollow metal cone mounted on a rod.

Capital (Latin *caput* – head) The head member surmounting a column*, usually ornamented. The style of the capital indicates the order* to which the column belongs.

Capsa Another name for a tabernacle*, though resembling a chest rather than a cupboard.

Cartouche An ornamental panel, often containing coats of arms or texts.

Catafalque A structure used to support a coffin at the Funeral Mass*.

Cathedra (Greek/Latin for 'chair') The seat of the bishop* in his cathedral*. The chair is the symbol of his duty to teach, rule and sanctify the Church* of his diocese*. The word originally referred to the chair used by ancient philosophers as a symbol of their authority.

Cathedral (Greek/Latin for 'chair') The church* where the bishop* has his seat. It is the principal church of the diocese* and a symbol of the 'local Church', the diocese, the basic unit of the Catholic* Church.

Cemetery (Greek *koimeterion* – a place to sleep) The site dedicated to the burial* of the dead.

Chair The seat for the priest* at Mass*, from which he may preach* the homily*.

Chancel (Latin *cancellum* – a screen or enclosure) That part of a church* usually known as the sanctuary* or altar*, originally screened off from the rest of the church.

Chantry (French *chanter* to sing) Originally a small chapel* endowed for a daily Mass* in memory of someone, where a priest* was paid to 'sing' Mass.

Chantry chapel See **Chantry**

Chapel A part of a church* which contains either a secondary altar*, or the Blessed Sacrament* or a shrine*. In the nineteenth century, Catholics* often described their churches as 'the chapel'.

Chapel of ease A church* building which is not a parish church, but which is situated to serve the needs of parishioners in outlying districts of a parish*.

Chapter house In cathedrals* or monasteries*, the room where the canons* or monks* met to do business. The meeting was begun with a short reading, or 'chapter', from Scripture*.

Chevron Romanesque* ornament in zigzag pattern, found on pillars* and arches.

Choir The part of a church* occupied by singers (alternative spelling *quire*).

Christmas crib a representation of Christ* as a baby in the manger. Saint Francis is supposed to have made the first crib at Greccio in 1223. Cribs are sometimes very elaborate, and in Italy often take the form of large tableaux with hundreds of figures of shepherds, houses, animals and landscapes. The crib is usually blessed* and 'opened' at Midnight Mass* of Christmas*.

Church, redundant Under ecclesiastical exemption*, a church* that the bishop* has declared to be no longer used for worship*.

Churchyard The grounds of a church*, usually walled. In old churches, the dead are buried in the churchyard.

Ciborium (Greek *kiborion* – a husk, shell or cup) A structure supported on columns* sheltering an altar*. Sometimes also referred to as the baldacchino*. The term is also used of a vessel used to carry the Blessed Sacrament*.

Classical orders The styles and designs of columns* and associated elements which typify the architecture of Greece and Rome and their revival in the sixteenth century and afterwards. They are usually classified as Tuscan* or Doric*, Ionic* and Corinthian*.

Clerestory The upper tier of windows in a church* immediately below the ceiling.

Cloister (Latin *clausura* – enclosure) In monasteries*, a square walkway set about a green, used for exercise and in some cases for study. The main rooms of the monastery usually open off the cloister.

Colonnade A row of columns*.

Column A freestanding pillar* with base, shaft* and capital*.

Confessional The place where the Sacrament of Penance* is celebrated. This may be a small room or wooden booth which allows the priest* and penitent* to communicate through a grille (or in some cases, face to face).

Conopaeum (Greek *konops* – a mosquito net) The veil* covering the tabernacle* where the Blessed Sacrament* is reserved.

Consecration cross At the dedication* of a church*, the walls are anointed with Chrism* in twelve or four places (symbolising the twelve Apostles* or the four Evangelists*). Small incised crosses* are placed there as a memorial of the dedication*, and on the dedication anniversary, they may be illuminated with candles*.

Corbel (Latin *corvus* – a raven) A projecting stone or stepped series of projections functioning as a bracket to support a beam or statue.

The classical orders: doric, ionic and corinthian

Corinthian order The third of the classical orders*, characterised by the elaborate foliage pattern on the capitals* of columns*.

Cornice (French) A projecting horizontal moulded course, usually the topmost member of the entablature*.

Corona (Latin for crown) In classical* architecture, the overhanging vertical member of the cornice*, above the entablature* and below the roof. Also used of a suspended circle or hoop of metal containing lights.

Cosmatesque A style of decoration consisting of circular, square or rectangular slices of precious marble set in mosaic. The Cosmati family were masters of the art in the twelfth century.

Credence (Latin *Credo* – the Creed) The table used for the sacred vessels before they are placed on the altar* at Mass*.

Crocket (Old French *crochet*) an ornamental projection on a spire* or pinnacle.

Cross (Latin *crux*) The Christian* symbol*, used to adorn churches*. In form it is stylised into several variants: Greek, with four equal arms, Latin, with the bottom arm lengthened, and other forms.

Crossing In a cruciform* church*, the meeting of nave*, transept* and chancel*.

Crucifix The cross* with the figure of Christ* crucified attached to it. Churches* will usually display a crucifix on the walls or carried in procession*.

Cruciform (Latin *crux* – a cross) Shaped like a cross*.

Crypt (Latin *crypta* – vault*) A chamber beneath a church*, entered from the interior, where relics* are venerated or burials* performed.

Curtilage (Medieval Latin *curtilagium*) The land surrounding a church* and recognised as belonging to it.

Cusp (Latin *cuspis* – spear point, apex) The intersection of two arcs in Gothic* window tracery*.

Decorated The style of church* building in the fourteenth century, characterised by elaborate flowing window tracery* and wall decoration. Many nineteenth-century churches also adopted this style.

Diaper A form of wall decoration with motifs framed in a repeated diamond grid pattern.

Dome A hemispherical or bowl-shaped roof structure, vault* or ceiling. The best-known examples are Saint Peter's Basilica* in Rome*, Saint Paul's Cathedral* in London and the Washington Capitol building.

Doric order The first of the classical orders*, characterised by a plain cushion capital* on fluted* columns*.

Dormer window A vertical window projecting from the slope of a roof under a small gable.

Dorsal (or dossal) a textile panel or curtain hung as a reredos* for an altar*.

Early English The style of church* building in the thirteenth century, characterised by long, narrow, pointed windows, later by larger, geometrically traceried windows, and some decoration. This style became very popular in the nineteenth century for church construction.

Ecclesiastical exemption The Church* in England and Wales is not required to seek local authority listed building consent to make certain alterations to historic ('listed') churches* or to buildings within the curtilage*. Parliament at present allows the Church to operate its own system of consent, by which works to a listed building must first receive a faculty* from the bishop*, who delegates his authority to an 'Historic Churches Committee.'

Ecclesiology The study of the building and adornment of churches*. The term is also used for the theology* of the Church*.

Effigy (Latin *effigies* – likeness) An image*, usually part of a funerary monument, but sometimes applied to statues of saints*.

Elevation The vertical view of a building.

Encaustic tile A ceramic tile with an applied design fixed by firing in a kiln.

Engaged column A column* attached to a wall, so that between half and three-quarters of its circumference may be seen.

Entablature The elaborated horizontal beam carried upon columns*, divided in classical* architecture into architrave*, frieze* and cornice*.

Epistle side A term formerly in use to denote the right-hand corner of the altar* where the Epistle* was read at Mass*.

Exedra In Romanesque* and Byzantine* churches*, a term for the apse*.

Faculty The formal permission granted by the diocesan bishop* to allow works to proceed on building or renovating a church*.

Faldstool (Latin *faldistorium* – a folding chair or camp stool) A moveable chair or kneeling desk, often the seat used by the bishop* when not at the cathedral*.

Fall A textile covering or ornament for an altar*, lectern* or pulpit*.

Fan vault A type of arched roof with ribs* of equal length which spring out from their supporting shafts* like the skeleton of a fan. Examples are at King's College Chapel*, Cambridge, and King Henry VII Chapel, Westminster Abbey.

Feretory (Latin *feretrum* – something carried) A casket containing the relics* of a saint*, sometimes placed in a shrine*.

Fillet (Latin *filum* – thread) A flat ornamental band used on wall surfaces and columns*.

Finial An ornament used to top off a roof, gable, pinnacle or canopy.

Fleche (French for 'arrow') A spire*, usually small and slender, rising from the roof of a church*.

Flute/fluted An ornamental groove or channel cut into the shaft* of a column*.

Flying buttress A buttress* in the form of an arch, to carry the thrust of a vault* onto the lower walls of a church*.

Font (Latin *fons* – a spring or well) The place of baptism* in churches*. It may take the form of a pool, or it can be a large bowl supported by a column*.

Footpace The step immediately in front of the altar* on which the priest* stands.

Frieze The middle part of the classical* entablature*.

Frontal An ornament of metal, stone or coloured cloth that covers the front and sometimes the sides and back of the *mensa** of the altar*. It is known also as the antependium*.

Funeral pall The white cloth which may cover the coffin at a funeral, intended as a reminder of the white garment given in baptism*.

Gallery An elevated space often at the rear of a church*, sometimes used for organ* and choir*, and supported on columns* or brackets.

Gargoyle (Old French *gargouille* – throat) A projecting water* spout, carved into grotesque human or animal shape.

Glory An almond-shaped nimbus*, often associated with figures of Christ* or Our Lady*.

Gospel side The left-hand end of a rectangular altar*, where in Low Mass* the Gospel* was read.

Gothic The pointed arch style, which emerged in Europe in the twelfth century, probably with Islamic precedents. The term 'Gothic' was coined in the classical* revival to demean medieval architecture as barbaric. The Goths were a barbarian tribe.

Gothic Revival The medieval pointed-arch style of building was revived in the eighteenth century as a romantic curiosity. Then in the nineteenth century, architects began to use it deliberately for churches in order to stress the continuity of the Church* with its medieval ancestor. Pointed arched churches were still being created up till the Second World War.

Gradine A step or shelf placed on or behind an altar*, used to place candlesticks and cross*.

Groin The edge formed by the intersection of two vaults*, or the continuous moulding* covering the join.

Grille An openwork metal screen.

Hall church A church* with nave* and aisles* of equal height.

Hanging pyx A vessel for the Blessed Sacrament* which is suspended over an altar*. It is occasionally seen in Catholic* churches*. See **Pyx**

Hassock A stiffened cushion for kneeling*.

Hearse (Medieval Latin *hirpex* – a rake or harrow) Originally a structure erected over a body at a funeral to support candles or a pall*. Now used of the car that transports coffins to the place of committal.

High altar The principal altar* of a church*.

Icon (Ikon) (Greek *eikon* – image) A two-dimensional image*, painted or carved, of a saint* or religious* episode. Icons are found in Catholic* and Orthodox* churches*.

Iconostasis The screen separating the sanctuary* from the nave* in churches* of the Byzantine Rite*.

Impost A stone placed above the capital* of a column* to take the thrust of the arches above.

Ionic order The second of the orders* of classical* architecture. It is defined by the curling scrolls at the sides of the capitals* of columns*.

Jerusalem cross A cross* associated with the Holy Sepulchre Church* in Jerusalem, having arms of equal length with small crosses inscribed in the angles of the arms.

Jesse window A window depicting Jesse, the ancestor of King David, and therefore of Jesus*, with a tree growing out of his loins on the branches of which are depicted his descendants.

King post A vertical post connecting the tie beam* to the apex of the rafters, in a roof truss.

Lady chapel A chapel* or shrine*, within a larger church*, set apart for devotion* to Our Lady*.

Lamp Lamps in Church* are used to indicate the presence of the Blessed Sacrament* in the tabernacle*. They may also burn before images* of saints*.

Lancet window (Latin *lancea* – a lance) A long, slender, pointed window.

Lantern (Latin *lanterna* – a light) A windowed structure on top of a gable, roof or dome*.

Latin cross A cross* having the lower arm longer than the other arms.

Lectern (Latin *legere* – to read) A stand with sloping shelf for books. Lecterns may be designed in the form of an eagle, or be portable, made to fold up like a deckchair.

Lierne vaulting Decorative rib* vaulting using non-structural ribs for ornamentation, characteristic of later medieval architecture.

Light (German *licht*, Latin *lux* – light) The division of a large Gothic* window.

Lintel (Old French *lintel* – threshold) A horizontal beam over an opening, carrying the weight of the wall above.

Lombard A style of round-arched building, based on medieval north Italian models.

Louvre Sloping slats, filling an opening. Often used in belfries*.

Lozenge (Medieval French *lozenge* – possibly a tombstone) An ornamental shield, used occasionally to display coats of arms in churches*.

Lych gate (German *Leiche* – corpse) The roofed gateway to a churchyard*, once used to shelter coffins during the funeral* service.

Memorial An object in a church* given in memory of someone.

Mensa (Latin *mensa* – table) The stone top of an altar*, marked with five crosses* and anointed with Chrism* at its dedication.

Misericord (Latin *misericordia* – pity) In medieval churches*, a seat which, when turned upright, formed a ledge, to support those standing during long services*. The support was often carved.

Mission architecture Eighteenth-century church* architecture of the Spanish religious* orders* in New Mexico and California.

Monument (Latin *monere* – to remind) A structure placed over a grave* to commemorate the person buried.

Mosaic Small cubes of coloured or glazed material forming a picture or design. Mosaic was extensively used in early Christian* art.

Moulding A decorative feature to introduce variety into any surface, particularly cornices* and columns*.

Mullion A vertical bar dividing areas in doors and windows.

Narthex (Greek *narthex* – a container) An enclosed lobby, situated at the entrance to a church* but separate from it.

Nave (Latin *navis* – a ship) The main space in a church* as distinct from the sanctuary*. The congregation* takes its place in the nave.

Norman The style of churches* built between 1066 and about 1170, characterised by round arches and use of the apse*. Some nineteenth-century churches were also built in this style.

Oratory A church* belonging to the Oratorian* order, founded in the sixteenth century by Saint Philip Neri. The word is also used for a smaller church, or chapel*, which is not a parish church*.

Order The distinctive types of classical* column* and entablature*.

Organ (Greek *organon* – tool) A mechanical musical instrument, either composed of many pipes, sounded by air pumped through, or of electronic units which simulate the pipe sounds.

Pall (Latin *pallium* – cloak) A cloth spread over a coffin at funerals*, usually white, so that it echoes the white cloth wrapped around a child at baptism*. The term is also used occasionally of a large tablecloth covering the altar* table on all sides to the ground.

Parclose (Old French *parclos* – shut off) An openwork screen or railings, often fencing a chapel* from the body of the church*.

Parvis/parvise (Latin *paradisus* – paradise) An open square in front of a large church*, or an enclosed anteroom within a church.

THE SANCTIFYING CHURCH

Paschal candle (Hebrew *Pesach* – Passover*)
The large candle*, blessed* at the Easter
Vigil*, which stands near the lectern* during
Easter* time until Pentecost*. It may be decorated with the date of the year, an alpha* and
omega*, and five pieces of incense* symbolising the wounds of Christ*. After Pentecost the
paschal candle is placed near the font*.

Pendentive The concave wall surface between
a dome* and its supporting masonry.

Perpendicular The last of the styles of medieval English Gothic*, characterised by large
windows with ranks of rectilinear tracery*,
sometimes also by fan vaulting*.

Pew (from Latin *podium* – platform) A bench
with back and somewhat enclosed ends which
provides seats for a congregation*. Pews began
to appear in churches* at the end of the thirteenth century.

The paschal candle

Pier A heavy column* or thickened wall section, designed to support a concentrated vertical weight.

Pilaster An engaged column* supporting a vertical weight, or a decorative feature
in the form of an engaged column.

Pillar A slender column*, supporting an arch* or architrave*.

Piscina (Latin for fish pool) A shallow basin with earth drain, projecting from
a wall or enclosed within a recess. It was used as a credence* table and to wash
the chalice* after Mass*.

Plinth The base of a column*, pilaster* or vertical moulding*.

Poppyhead (French *poupee* – a doll) The carved apex of a pew* end, often in
human or animal form.

Porch The covered entry way to a church*.

Portico (Latin *porticus*, from *porta* – door) A grand porch, or roof supported on
columns* at the entrance of a church*.

Predella The platform or footpace* in front of the altar*, or the bottom tier of
a large altarpiece*.

Pricket A candlestick with a spike to hold the candle*.

Prie-Dieu (French for pray God) A portable kneeling* desk.

Processional cross The cross* used in processions* and placed near the altar*
during the Mass*. It must have a figure of the crucified Christ* on it.

Pulpit (Latin *pulpitum* – a raised platform) An elevated enclosed stand used for
preaching*. Pulpits were a significant feature of churches* from their origin in
the Middle Ages until the last century. They are less used nowadays, as the
homily* is delivered from the priest's* chair or lectern*.

Purlin A piece of timber laid horizontally along the rafters to support the roof
boards under the outer covering.

Pyx A vessel used to reserve the Blessed Sacrament*. The pyx was sometimes
suspended above the altar*, or rested upon it as the ancestor of the modern
tabernacle*.

Quoin (French *coin* – corner) A square or rectangular stone used to make the
corner of a building.

Rafter A sloping timber, supporting a roof covering.

Relic A portion of a saint's* body or clothing kept for veneration. Relics are usually placed beneath the altar* during the dedication* ritual.

Reliquary A vessel containing relics*.

Rendering The coat of plaster or other material applied to a wall surface.

Renovation See re-ordering below.

Re-ordering The process of renovating a church* interior (moving the altar*, font* and other objects) to suit changing fashions in liturgical* celebration*.

Reredos (*rere* – behind, and French *dos* – back) The ornamental panel set behind an altar, when the altar* is set against a wall.

Retable A reredos* composed of carved or painted panels set within a frame.

Reveal The sides of a window or door opening in the thickness of a wall.

Rib The curved structural member that acts as part of a 'skeleton' separating the panels of a vault*.

Riddel (French *rideau* – curtain) In medieval churches*, the curtain that hung at the sides and back of an altar*.

Romanesque A style of architecture characterised by round arches, barrel* vaulting and smaller windows. It was the style employed in church* architecture in the early medieval period until the middle of the twelfth century.

Rood (Old English *rod* – cross*) The great crucifix* which was set up over the entrance to the chancel*, or suspended over the altar*.

Rood loft The gallery supported by the rood screen*, often used by singers in the Middle Ages.

Rood screen In medieval and Gothic Revival* churches*, the screen* separating nave* from chancel*, sometimes supporting the rood*.

Rose window A circular window with tracery* resembling the petals of a rose. The term often refers generally to any large circular window.

Sacrament house The name usually given to a free-standing structure for the reservation of the Blessed Sacrament* when it is not a tabernacle*.

Sacrarium The place where holy water*, or other blessed* liquids, may be disposed of to allow them to drain away into the earth.

Sacred vessels The chalice* and paten* used in the celebration of Mass.

Sacristy (Latin *sacer* – holy) The room where sacred vessels and vestments* are stored and prepared.

Saddle roof A roof with two gables and one ridge, suggestive of a saddle.

Sanctuary (Latin *sanctus* – holy*) That part of a church* which contains the altar*. The term may be used also to refer to the whole of a church building.

Sanctuary step The area where the altar* stands in a church building must be marked off from the rest of the space. This is usually achieved by a step to raise the altar area.

Sconce The part of a candlestick that takes the drips and holds the candle* itself.

Screen A partition dividing one part of a church* from the rest of the building.

Sedilia (Latin *sedile* – seat) Architectural seats for the clergy*, set in the right-hand wall of the chancel*.

Shaft The middle part of a column*, between the base and the capital*.

Shrine (Latin *scrinium* – a box) Originally a reliquary*, now used to describe part of a church*, apart from the main body of the building, dedicated to prayer*.

Slype A narrow passage between two buildings, often within the thickness of a wall.

Soffit (Latin *suffixus* – fastened beneath) The underside of an arch or beam.

Sounding board A canopy, usually over a pulpit*, to direct the sound of the voice into the congregation*.

Spandrel On a wall surface, the angle between the side of an arch and the vertical, or the space between the curvature of two neighbouring arches.

Spire A slender conical or needle construction surmounting a building.

Stained glass Transparent or translucent glass, coloured during manufacture (as opposed to painted), used ornamentally in windows.

Stall A fixed seat, for the use of clergy* or choir*. Stalls are often elaborately ornamented. If it had a tip-up seat, this was known as a misericord*.

Stations of the Cross (Latin *statio* – a halt on a march) A series of numbered plaques around the walls of a church*, used for the service* known as the Way of the Cross*. The stations may be painted with the episode commemorated.

Steeple A tall ornamental structure such as a tower* and spire.*

Stoup An ornamental basin near the door of a church* containing holy water* for people to sprinkle themselves on entering and leaving the church.

String course A horizontal decorative moulding* on a wall, usually projecting from the surface.

Stucco A mixture of cement, lime and sand used to render external walls, often applied ornamentally, or any ornamental interior plaster design.

Tabernacle The vessel used to reserve the Blessed Sacrament*. It is shaped like a small safe, sometimes with a dome or conical cover, and standing on a pedestal in a chapel* set apart for the purpose of reservation*. The tabernacle may also stand in the sanctuary* where appropriate. It should be covered with a conopaeum* or veil*.

Tabernacle work A decorated screen* with niches for sculpture.

Tablet A small slab or panel placed on a wall as a memorial*.

Tester A flat canopy, usually suspended from the ceiling, over an altar*.

Throne The place where the monstrance* is placed for Exposition of the Blessed Sacrament*. The term was formerly used to describe the cathedra* of the bishop*.

Tomb (Medieval Latin *tumba* – a burial mound) A place for burial* of the dead, usually an ornamental structure above or below ground.

Tower (Latin *turris*) A tall structure, square or circular, forming part of a church* or other building, or standing independently of it.

Tracery The stonework in the head of a large Gothic* window, dividing it into smaller areas of glazing. In Gothic* architecture, windows have elaborate tracery.

Transept (Latin *trans* – across, and *septum* – enclosure) The arms of a cruciform* church*, set at right angles to the main axis.

Transom (Latin *trans* – across) A horizontal bar of wood or stone dividing a large window.

Triforium In a medieval church*, the floor or gallery above the main arcade*, usually itself arcaded. It may form an upper walkway around the church.

Triptych (Greek *tri* – three, and *ptusso* – I fold) A series of three painted or carved panels linked by hinges and able to be displayed open or closed. Large altarpieces* are often constructed in this form.

Truss A rigid triangular frame of wood or metal supporting a roof.

Tuscan order A Roman form of the Greek Doric order*.

Tympanum (Greek *tumpanon* – drum) The flat surface filling an arch when there is a rectangular door lintel below it. The tympanum is often ornamented.

Undercroft The vaulted basement of a church*, known also as a crypt*.

Vane A metal plate set on a spindle to allow it to turn and show the wind direction.

Vault (Latin *volvere* – to roll) An arched ceiling. The term is also used to denote an underground burial* place.

Vesica An elongated oval or almond-shaped form, usually employed as a surround for an image* of Christ* or Our Lady*.

Vestry The room in a church* where vestments* are put on. It may also be known as the sacristy*.

Voussoir (Latin *volvere* – to roll) A wedge-shaped masonry block in an arch or vault*.

Wagon roof A barrel vault*, a continuous semicircular ceiling.

Wall plate The horizontal timber beam which extends along the length of a wall beneath the roof.

Weathercock A weathervane* shaped like a cockerel.

Weathervane See **Vane**

Wheel window A large circular window with radiating spoke tracery*, having the appearance of a wheel.

Wrought ironwork Iron hammered or forged when incandescent, to form ornamental shapes.

MUSIC IN THE LITURGY

Liturgical* singing is as old as the Church*. It may be descended from Jewish liturgical song. For hundreds of years (and still in many of the Eastern Churches*) no instruments were used. In Europe in the late Middle Ages the organ* began to develop as an instrument for accompanying the song of the liturgy. Other instruments followed, and music became more complex, until in the eighteenth century church music was almost indistinguishable from opera. More recently, the Liturgical Movement* and the reforms called for by the Second Vatican Council* have encouraged a return to simpler, more congregational forms.

After the Second Vatican Council the place of song in the liturgy was made more important. The ministry* of the cantor* was encouraged. Collections of simple chants both in Latin and the vernacular were issued. The vernacular Mass* at first borrowed many hymns* from other Christian* traditions*, but soon new compositions appeared specifically composed to suit the more responsorial* style of liturgical singing.

The Mass may be sung in several ways. A fully sung Mass would have all the prayers* of the priest* sung as well as singing at the beginning, between the readings, at the offertory*, the acclamations* in the Eucharistic Prayer* and at communion*. Most Masses do not achieve this but it is usual to have some singing, at least at Sunday* Mass.

The Liturgy of the Hours* may be sung with similar degrees of musical elaboration, though this is rarely achieved outside monastic communities.

Word List

A cappella (Italian for 'according to the custom of the chapel*') Unaccompanied choral song.

Acclamation A short text, sung as part of the liturgy*. The 'Holy Holy Holy'* and 'Christ* has died . . .' in the Eucharistic Prayer* are acclamations.

Adoro Te (full line *Adoro te devote, latens Deitas* – I adore you devoutly, hidden Divinity) A medieval Latin eucharistic* hymn*.

Agnus Dei 'Lamb of God*, you take away the sins* of the world, have mercy on us . . . grant us peace' The litany* sung during the breaking of the bread* at Mass*.

Alleluia The Greek and Latin form of the Hebrew acclamation* 'Hallelujah' meaning 'Praise God*!' The Alleluia is sung at Mass* before the reading of the Gospel*.

Amen (Hebrew for 'truly' or 'yes!') An acclamation* taken over by the Church* in apostolic* times from the synagogue. It is used in Judaism, Christianity and Islam as an affirmation at the end of prayer*.

Anthem (Latin *antiphona* – antiphon*) A piece sung by a choir*.

Antiphon (Latin *antiphona* – singing by two choirs* in alternation) A short text sung before, sometimes during and after, a psalm* or canticle* as a sort of refrain.

Antiphonale Monasticum 'The Monastic Antiphon Book' – the book containing the music for the Liturgy of the Hours* for monks* who follow the Rule of Saint Benedict*.

Antiphonale Romanum 'The Roman Antiphon Book' – the book containing the music for the Liturgy of the Hours* in the Roman Rite*.

Antiphoner (Latin *antiphonale*) The book containing the music for the Divine Office*.

Benedictus 'Blessed* is he who comes in the name of the Lord*' The second half of the acclamation* 'Holy Holy Holy'* in the Eucharistic Prayer* at Mass*. The Benedictus is also the Canticle* of Zechariah (Luke* 1:67–79) sung at Lauds*.

Canon A round, with each part entering at different times and thus singing the melody polyphonically.

Cantata (Latin *cantare* – to sing) A musical work consisting of solo recitatives and arias, concluded by a chorale. The origin of the name is Latin – *Missa cantata*, the 'sung Mass* out of which the cantata developed in the seventeenth century.

Canticle (Latin *canticum* – a song) Certain texts from Scripture* and Church* tradition* that are sung in a similar way to the psalms*.

Cantillation The chanting* of a prayer* or Scripture* text by a soloist, often the presiding priest* or other minister*.

Cantor (Latin *cantare* – to sing) A song leader who sings verses* to which the congregation* replies with a refrain or antiphon*.

Carol (from Greek *choros* – dance) A popular folk song with a dance-like melody. Carols are associated with Christmas* and other great festivals*. The term is now used for any Christmas song.

Chant/chanting (Latin *cantus* – a song) A way of singing a text, usually associated with an ancient, sacred or modal* musical form.

Choir (Latin *chorus* – body of singers) A group of ministers* whose task is to lead and support sung liturgy*, and occasionally to perform on their own.

Communion The name given to an antiphon* sung as people approach the altar* in procession* for Holy Communion*.

Credo (Latin for 'I believe') The Profession of Faith* or creed*. The Nicene Creed* and the Apostles' Creed* may both be used at Mass*.

Doxology (Greek *doxologia* – glorification) A prayer* of praise, at the end of certain prayers (such as 'through him, with him, in him . . .' at the end of the Eucharistic Prayer*) and also the verse* repeated at the conclusion of psalms*: 'Glory be to the Father and to the Son and to the Holy Spirit'. Hymns* may also end with a doxology.

Exsultet (Latin *Exsultet iam angelica turba caelorum* – 'Let the heavenly angel throng rejoice') The blessing* chanted* at the beginning of the Easter Vigil*.

Gloria in excelsis See **Glory to God in the highest**

Gloria Patri (Latin 'Glory be to the Father*') See **Glory be**

Glory be The doxology* 'Glory be to the Father* and to the Son* and to the

Holy Spirit*, as it was in the beginning, is now and ever shall be, world without end, Amen*.' It is said after recitation of a psalm* and at other times (such as part of the Our Father*, Hail Mary* and Glory be set of prayers*).

Glory to God in the highest An ancient Trinitarian hymn* sung at the beginning of Mass* on Sundays* (except in Advent* and Lent*).

Graduale Romanum (Roman Gradual) (Latin *gradus* – step) The book containing all the Ordinary* and Proper* chants* for the Mass*. Issued first in 1908 by Pope* Pius X, reformed after the Second Vatican Council* and re-issued by Pope Paul VI in 1974.

Graduale Simplex (Simple Gradual) (Latin *gradus* – step) A book of simple Latin chants* for Mass*. published in 1967 (revised in 1974).

A line of Gregorian chant

Gregorian chant The chant* of the Latin liturgy*. The body of chant is by legend ascribed to Saint* Gregory the Great (Pope* CE590–604). It is also known as plainsong*.

Holy Holy Holy English translation of the *Sanctus** acclamation* in the Eucharistic Prayer*.

Hymn (Greek *hymnos*) A liturgical* text intended for singing. It may be in prose or verse, though nowadays we associate the term with rhymed verses. Hymns have been sung in the prayer* of the Church* since the time of Saint Paul*, who quotes lines from contemporary hymns. Saint Ambrose is said to have written the first verse hymns. In the Latin liturgy*, hymns are not usually sung at Mass*, though they are sung in vernacular Masses.

Intone (Latin *intonare* – to sound) To chant* a text.

Introit (Latin *introire* – to come in) The verses* of a psalm* which serve as the music for the entrance procession* at Mass*. At Mass without singing, the verses may be recited.

Kyrie eleison (Greek *Kyrios* – Lord, and *eleison* – have mercy) An acclamation* addressed to Christ*, the Lord*. It is used at the beginning of Mass*, in the Liturgy of the Hours* and in the Litany of the Saints*.

Liber Cantualis (Latin *liber* – a book, and *cantus* – a song) The collection of simple plainsong* pieces published in 1978 by the Abbey* of Solesmes*.

Liber Usualis (Latin *liber* – a book, and *usus* – custom) The book of Latin chant* for Mass* and the Hours first published by the Benedictine* monastery* of Solesmes* in 1896, revised in 1903, 1934, 1955 and 1963.

Magnificat (Latin *magnificare* – to give glory) The first words of the Virgin* Mary's* hymn* 'My soul* glorifies the Lord*' in Luke* 1:46–55. The Magnificat is used at Vespers*.

Modal (Latin *modus* – manner) Of or pertaining to musical modes*. A form of music found in all ancient Church* chant*, and in folksong.

Mode (Latin *modus* – manner) In Gregorian chant* there are usually held to be eight musical modes, each with a series of typical melodies.

Motet (Italian *motetto* – a movement) A short choral piece to cover actions at Mass* such as the preparation of the altar*.

Nunc dimittis (Latin for 'Now you dismiss') The song of Simeon, 'Lord* now you let your servant go in peace', in Luke* 2:29–32. It is used at Compline*.

O Antiphons Special antiphons* to the Magnificat* for Vespers* on the days preceding Christmas*. Each addresses Christ* in the language of the Old Testament* prophecies, beginning with 'O'.

Offertory The Latin chant* that accompanies the preparation of the altar* at Mass*.

Office hymn A hymn* appropriate to the time of day or the feast*, sung at the Liturgy of the Hours*.

Oratorio A semi-dramatised musical piece often on sacred themes for soloists, chorus and orchestra. The name comes from the Oratory* of Saint Philip Neri in Italy in the sixteenth century where such pieces were first performed.

O Salutaris (full line: *O salutaris hostia* – O saving Sacrifice) The last two verses of a medieval eucharistic* hymn* often sung at Benediction*.

Plainsong The usual English term ('plain', i.e., without harmony) for Gregorian chant*.

Polyphony Harmonised singing. The term is usually associated with the sixteenth-century Renaissance composers.

Precentor (Latin *prae* – in front of, and *canere* – to sing) The musician responsible for leading the chant* and directing the music in cathedral* and monastic* churches.

Psalm (Greek *psalmos*) A liturgical* song from the Book of Psalms* in the Old Testament*.

Psalmody The singing or recitation of psalms*; also the collection of psalms appointed for each part of the Liturgy of the Hours*.

Psalter The Book of Psalms*, or the psalms and canticles* for use at the Liturgy of the Hours*.

Response (Latin *respondere* – to answer) The people's answer to liturgical* greetings or directions.

Responsorial (Latin *respondere* – to answer) A way of singing involving the cantor* who sings lines then repeated by the congregation*.

Responsorial psalm The psalm* or canticle* that follows the first reading at Mass* It may be sung as cantor's* verses* with refrain, all through by the congregation*, or all through by a soloist.

Responsory (Latin *respondere* – to answer) A set of scriptural verses used as a response* to a reading.

Salve Regina ('Hail, holy Queen') The prayer* to Our Lady* recited at the end of Compline*.

Sanctus (Latin for 'holy*') 'Holy, Holy, Holy* Lord*' The first people's acclamation* in the Eucharistic Prayer*.

Sequence (Latin *sequentia* – what follows) A metrical hymn* sometimes sung before the Gospel* on great feasts*. There were many sequences in medieval liturgy*, but fewer in the modern Roman Missal*. Among the best known are *Victimae Paschali Laudes* ('Christians, give thanks to the Paschal* Victim') for Easter*, *Veni Sancte Spiritus* ('Come, Holy Spirit*') for Pentecost* and *Dies Irae* ('O day of wrath'), formerly used at the Requiem Mass*.

Solesmes The Benedictine* monastery* founded in 1832 by Prosper Gueranger in France, which was influential in the restoration of Gregorian chant* in the Catholic* Church*. With its traditions of scholarship, Solesmes has been responsible to the Holy See* for the preparation of the recognised editions of Latin plainsong* since the end of the nineteenth century.

Taize The music of the Ecumenical* Community at Taize, France, has become popular in recent years in Catholic* liturgy*. Much of it consists of short harmonised chants* or refrains, repeated many times to allow the words to become prayer*.

Tantum ergo (full line: *Tantum ergo sacramentum veneremur cernui* – So great a sacrament* therefore let us adore) The concluding verses of a medieval eucharistic* hymn*, sung at Benediction*.

Te Deum laudamus (Latin for 'We praise you, O God*') The hymn* sung at the conclusion of the Office of Readings* on Sundays* and holy days*. It is ascribed to Nicetas, Bishop* of Remesiana in the fifth century CE.

Tone (Latin *tonus* – tune) The simple chant*, consisting of a reciting note and ornamental ending, used to sing the psalms*.

Tract (Latin *tractus* – something drawn out or elaborated) A type of psalm* chant* at Mass* once used between the readings during Lent*. The tract is characterised by highly ornamented music.

Trope (Greek *tropos* – an elaboration) A text used to ornament another text. The *Kyrie eleison** (Lord* have mercy) is sometimes 'troped', as in 'You were sent to heal the contrite, Lord have mercy'.

Veni Creator (Latin for 'Come, Creator Spirit*') The Latin hymn* for Pentecost*, written probably in the eighth century, now used as the hymn for Vespers* between Ascension* and Pentecost and at other times of solemn prayer*.

Verse For recitation and singing, the psalms* are divided into verses, of two or more lines with a division in the middle. In reciting the psalms, two groups of people will recite alternate verses.

Versicles and responses (Latin *versiculi* – verses) Short verses, usually from the psalms, recited at the Divine Office*.

SACRED SCRIPTURE

The Scriptures are the witness to God's* calling of a chosen people and the universality of that calling for all peoples in Jesus* Christ*, by the power of the Holy Spirit*.

The Church* understands the Scriptures as 'inspired', that is, as testimony to the authentic purposes and word* of God. The Church understands Scripture as the most important element in the tradition* of faith*. The faith of the Church has to agree with Scripture.

The Church engages with the word of God through the proclamation of the Scriptures in the liturgy* and its own ritual* response* in the responsorial psalm*, homily*, acclamations* and liturgical* prayer*. In addition, Scripture is used as part of personal prayer. The process known as *Lectio divina** (Latin for 'holy reading') is a slow reading, repetition and contemplation of Scripture.

For centuries the Scriptures were written in separate books. Later on, especially with the coming of printing, it became possible to create 'the Bible'* – the collection of all the Scriptures in one volume. This changed people's appreciation of the Scriptures. They began to be thought of as one single infallible *book* rather than as 'the word of the Lord' to be spoken.

This section will list the books accepted by the Catholic* Church as 'canonical'* – that is, having the authority of the whole Church. In each case a brief description of the book in terms of content, literary form and history will be given.

The Old Testament

The Pentateuch (Greek for 'five-fold scroll')

The first five books of the Hebrew Scriptures: Genesis*, Exodus*, Leviticus*, Numbers*, Deuteronomy* from the Jewish *Torah*, the 'Law'. These books are attributed to Moses, though their dates, origins and internal make-up are more complex.

Dating the Pentateuch is difficult, but in general terms, scholars think that these books reached their present form in the fourth century BCE. Underlying them are four older traditions, known as 'J' (Jahwist), 'E' (Elohist), 'D' (Deuteronomist) and 'P' (Priestly). The 'J' and 'E' traditions each use a different name for God* – 'Jahweh' and 'Elohim' respectively. They are tentatively dated in the tenth and ninth centuries BCE. The 'D' and 'P' traditions are later, being dated around the seventh to the fifth centuries BCE.

Genesis (Greek for 'becoming'. The Hebrew title is *Bereshith* – from the opening words of the book, 'In the beginning . . .') Genesis records the myths of creation, of human origins, primordial human strife, and the tale of the Flood. The larger and most ancient part of the book records the lives of Abraham, Isaac and Jacob, until the death of Joseph in Egypt. Genesis is a collection of ancient traditions* and myths, assembled at a later date. From Genesis, the Church* takes its teaching about God* and creation – that God is not part of the universe but its loving Creator from nothing – and the Fall* and the covenants* made before Moses.

Exodus (Greek for 'journey out') Exodus records the suffering of the Israelites in Egypt, their escape from Pharaaoh under Moses, the giving of the Ten Commandments* and the Law, and the journey towards the Land of Promise. The text has elements both from ancient tradition* and later practice, reflecting a more settled, agricultural, way of life in Canaan. From Exodus, the Church* took the Passover* narrative (Exodus 12) as symbolic of Christ*, the Passover Lamb, and the crossing of the Red Sea (Exodus 14) as a prototype of baptism*.

Leviticus (From Levi, the originator of the Temple priesthood*) Leviticus appears to be a collection of ritual* directions dating probably from the time of Moses until the settlement of Canaan. It expands the notion of 'holiness' – the holy* God* calling on his people to be holy, by detailed rules about priestly duties, sacrifice*, and in particular the Day of Atonement*.

Numbers (Named from its account of census materials and genealogies) The Book of Numbers contains further accounts of the life of Moses, the journey in the desert towards Canaan and some narratives concerning the events immediately prior to the entry into the Land. It is thought that the Evangelist* Matthew* probably took his account of the star which guided the Magi* to Jesus* (Matthew 2:1–10) from Numbers 24:17, the story of Balaam the wizard.

Deuteronomy (Greek *deutero* – second, and *nomos* – law) This later account of the Law may be the book whose discovery is recorded in 2 Chronicles 34:14ff. at the time of the reforms under King Josiah (*c.*621BCE). It contains a speech of Moses concerning fidelity to the covenant*.

Later History

Joshua Named after Moses' successor as leader, this book tells of the arrival of God's people in Canaan. It tells of the sacking of the cities of Jericho (where the walls fall down) and Ai (in fact destroyed long before, but these stories grew up to explain the ruins), the defeat of the Canaanites and the settlement of the Land. Approximate date of Joshua: early seventh century BCE.

Judges Judges covers the period between the settlement and the beginning of the monarchy under Saul. It is a reflection on the folly of worshipping other gods. Under the Judges (including Deborah, Gideon, Jephthah and Samson) Israel is continuously occupied by foreign powers (the Philistines) and set free by the Judges who recall the people to worship* of God*. Well-known stories include Gideon's revolt and Samson and Delilah. Approximate date of Judges: early seventh century BCE.

Ruth A novel, romance or love story. Ruth, a foreigner, the widow of an Israelite, enters the religion* of Israel, and marries Boaz, an Israelite. By this marriage*, she becomes an ancestor of King David. The date of the book is disputed, but could be anytime after *c.*800BCE.

1 Samuel Samuel is God's* choice as prophet* in Israel. The book recounts his miraculous birth, his calling by God as a small boy, his anointing first of Saul, then of David, as king. The rest of the book recounts Saul's reign, his jealousy of David and his death in battle. The stories of David and Goliath, and David and Jonathan are found in this book. Approximate date: later seventh century BCE.

2 Samuel This book covers the reign of David as king both in the Southern Kingdom of Judaea and the Northern Kingdom of Israel, his plan to build a temple and the rebellion of his son Absalom. Approximate date: later seventh century BCE.

1 Kings The history is continued with David's death and the reign of Solomon his son. Solomon builds the Temple, but then is unfaithful to God*. His death precipitates a division in the Kingdom, with Israel (the North) rebelling against Solomon's son Rehoboam. The cycle of stories associated with King Ahab, Queen Jezebel and the efforts of the Prophet* Elijah to uphold the cult of the Lord* forms the remainder of the book. Well-known stories include the Judgement of Solomon; Elijah and the prophets of Baal. Approximate date: later seventh century BCE.

2 Kings The story of the Israelite monarchy continues down to the fall of Samaria (721BCE). In Judah, King Josiah reforms the state and the Temple cult and discovers the Book of the Law (Deuteronomy*). The history of Judah is continued down to the final fall of Jerusalem and the exile of the people to Babylon in 586BCE. Approximate date: early sixth century BCE.

1 Chronicles The first part of one book containing all of Chronicles, Ezra* and Nehemiah*. This book covers the same general ground as the books of Kings*, but from a more Temple-based perspective. Approximate dating for Chronicles, Ezra and Nehemiah: the middle of the fourth century BCE.

2 Chronicles The history is continued from Solomon to the exile in Babylon.

Ezra The first part of the book gives an account of Ezra, the scribe who returned to Jerusalem after the release of the Jewish exiles under King Cyrus of Persia (539BCE) and of the rebuilding of the Temple. The second part, perhaps some fifty years later, tells of a second return of Jewish exiles in 457BCE.

Nehemiah The story of Nehemiah, cupbearer to Artaxerxes, King of Persia, commissioned by him to rebuild the walls of Jerusalem and reform the religious* cult.

Tales of Adventure and Romance

Tobit The Book of Tobit is a fictional (and very readable) tale about perseverance and fidelity to the Law and good works. It is set during the Jewish exile in Persia and concerns Tobit and his son, Tobias, who sets out to find a wife with the help of the Angel* Raphael. The book contains some beautiful passages about marriage*. Approximate date: the third century BCE.

Judith 'Judith' means 'Jewess' – she is a personification of her people and, like Esther* later on, their saviour. The story of Judith is set in the reign of King Nebuchadnezzar of Babylon. His general, Holofernes, threatens to invade Israelite territory. The book tells how he is assassinated by Judith, who makes her way into Holofernes' camp and seduces him with her beauty. Approximate date: the second century BCE.

Esther This story is set among those Jews who did not return from Babylon. Esther, adopted daughter of Mordechai, becomes the favoured wife of King Ahasuerus (Xerxes) and risks her own life to report to him a plot, formed by

Haman, an enemy of Mordecai, to destroy the Jewish people. She is successful and her people survive. Approximate date: second century BCE.

1 Maccabees The two books of Maccabees (Hebrew for 'the hammers') record the resistance of Jews to the hellenising Syrian kings in the second century BCE. The resistance is led by Mattathias and his sons. The style of the books is more Greek than Hebrew, but the message – fidelity to the *Torah* to the end – is thoroughly Jewish.

2 Maccabees Covering the same period as the first book, Second Maccabees has a more literary tone, and reads more like an edifying tale than a history. It is important for later Judaism and Christianity in that it deals with ideas such as creation out of nothing (7:28), prayer* for the dead (12:38) and the intercession* of the saints* (15:14). It was written in Greek, probably in the late second century BCE.

Wisdom Literature

With the exception of the Psalms*, the books from Job* to Ecclesiasticus* are collectively known as 'Wisdom Literature'. This is a type of contemplative writing, containing much practical wisdom in the form of short sayings or proverbs. Later Wisdom traditions concentrate on God's* activity in the world under the guise of 'Wisdom', a feminine semi-divine figure, who inspires wise men and women in understanding. The Church* has made use of the figure of Wisdom as a prototype of Christ*, the 'Wisdom of God'.

Job Job is two fictional tales juxtaposed, part two set within part one. The first part (chapters 1 and 2:1–11 and 42:10–17) is an ancient Middle Eastern tale of a rich man who loses everything, resigns himself to the will of God* and has his wealth restored. Between these two sections is the story of the debate between Job and his friends Eliphaz, Bildad, Zophar and (later) Elihu. They try to persuade him that his woes are not accidental, but the result of his own sinfulness. Job protests his innocence and calls on God to vindicate him. In a powerful ending, God appears as a whirlwind and berates Job on his human limitations. Job repents of his rash speech. Approximate date for Job: fifth century BCE.

Psalms This collection of liturgical* and devotional songs is associated with the Temple rebuilt after the Babylonian exile. It is in fact a combination of five books of songs and prayers*, each ending with a doxology* (Psalms 1–41; 42–72; 73–89; 90–106; 107–50) and ascribed to various authors, including King David. Characterised by imaginative colour and passion, the Psalms include great hymns* to God* the Creator (Psalm 104) and Liberator (Psalms 114, 116) together with prayers of great tenderness and insight (Psalms 23, 51, 90, 139). The collection may have been completed by the beginning of the second century BCE.

Proverbs A collection of sayings, both long and short, attributed to Solomon. Similar sayings have been discovered in Egypt and throughout the Middle East. The Proverbs deal with practical ways of pleasing God* by being attentive to the teaching of elders. Possible date: beginning of the fourth century BCE.

Ecclesiastes The work of a writer living in Jerusalem, with an ironic and fatalist worldview. Time is repetitive, freedom of little account, life is empty and death* certain. Possible date: middle of the third century BCE.

Song of Solomon A collection of erotic love poetry, praising the beauty of creation and the richness of human passion. Attributed to Solomon, but probably not by him. Jewish tradition* uses this as a book to be read at Passover*. Christian* tradition, more coy about its erotic overtones, treats it as a symbolic picture of Christ* and his bride, the Church*, or a poem about Christ's mystical courtship of the individual soul*. Possible date: fifth or fourth century BCE.

Wisdom A book written in Greek, not Hebrew. It originates almost certainly in Alexandria, from the Greek-speaking Jewish community there. Also unusual is its portrayal of Wisdom as a semi-divine being, God's* agent in the world, sharing intimately in God's nature. Probable date: some time in the first century BCE.

Ecclesiasticus (Sirach) Attributed to Ben Sira, a scribe of Jerusalem, and later translated into Greek (the book only survives as a whole in Greek), Ecclesiasticus (the term means a temple/synagogue official) writes about life from the perspective of mortality as a moment of judgement. Probable date of the Hebrew original: beginning of the second century BCE, and the Greek translation in 132BCE.

The Prophets

Prophets were inspired speakers with a divine message. Prophecy in ancient Israel was not confined to the written prophets. Elijah was a prophet, so was Elisha. Prophets saw through the culture of their day and attempted to recall the people to worship* and serve the One God*, when they had succumbed to the temptation to worship the gods of the land of Canaan.

The major prophets emerged in the political turmoil of the century and a half preceding the destruction of Jerusalem in 586BCE. Amos* and Hosea* in Israel, and Jeremiah* in the Southern Kingdom of Judah, accused the people of infidelity. The later prophets of the post-586BCE exile (Isaiah*, Ezekiel*) spoke of how God had punished the people for their infidelity and how God would reconcile them again.

Isaiah Three separate collections of prophecy, spanning some 300 years, go to make up Isaiah.

First Isaiah (Isaiah chapters 1–39) is the work of someone who began prophesying in the year that King Uzziah died (c.740BCE). This series of prophecies continues throughout the reigns of Jotham, Ahaz and into that of Hezekiah. The collection therefore covers a century and a half between c.600 and 450BCE. During those years, the Northern Kingdom of Israel was overrun by the Assyrians, who menaced the Southern Kingdom of Judah also. Isaiah and his disciples* saw the corruption of the nation's religion*, and spoke of the survival of a faithful 'remnant' whose sole hope* would be in God's* promises. Isaiah prophesied that a King would arise from David's line, a 'Messiah' (or 'Anointed One'*). The Church* has used Isaiah extensively, as foreshadowing the coming of Christ*.

Second Isaiah (Isaiah chapters 40–55) The unknown author, contemporary with Cyrus King of Persia (c.540BCE), offers a message of consolation for Jerusalem and promises a time of restoration. But the particular character of 'second Isaiah' is his universalism. The four 'Songs of the Servant' 42:1–9, 49:1–6, 50:4–11 and 52:13–53:12) appear to speak of a mysterious individual who by his witness of suffering will reveal God* for the whole world, not for the Jews only. These songs were crucial for the Church* in its deepening understanding of Jesus'* mission.

Third Isaiah (Isaiah 56–66) continues the themes of Second Isaiah. This collection probably emerged around 450BCE.

Jeremiah Born in about 645BCE, Jeremiah is perhaps the most appealing of the prophets*. He saw himself as a man of peace caught up in war, one not used to uttering messages of disaster. However, from his birth, his life and ministry* were dominated by the deteriorating situation that marked the end of the Kingdoms of Israel and Judah and the destruction of Jerusalem. Jerusalem fell in 597 to Nebuchadnezzar King of Babylon, who ten years later destroyed it and its Temple. Despite this, Jeremiah is not a prophet of doom, but of a good God* who wants to make a new covenant* with all people, 'written upon the heart' (chapter 31).

Lamentations Attributed to Jeremiah*, this is a collection of five poems describing the ruin of Jerusalem after its destruction by Nebuchadnezzar in 586BCE. Despite the title, a strong faith* in the providence* of God* emerges from the text. The Latin-speaking Church* has often used these poems as part of the Holy Week* liturgy*.

Baruch Baruch was Jeremiah's* secretary, but the book is much later, probably from the first century BCE. Four pieces make up the book, two in prose and two poems. It is a work of spirituality in exile and devotion* to the *Torah*.

Ezekiel Ezekiel was a visionary prophet*, living at the time of the destruction of Jerusalem in 586BCE, and sharing the exile of his people in Babylon. In a series of apocalyptic* images he describes his experience of the presence of God*, as he had received them in Babylon. His message was to prophesy the restoration of Israel and the rebuilding of the Temple. He saw the exilic community becoming the heart of the new nation through their conversion* of heart. He describes this process in images of dry bones coming to life and a flood of cleansing waters*, to make a new and holy* nation. The probable date for our present text of Ezekiel is about the middle of the fifth century BCE.

Daniel This book was written during the persecution of the Jews (and the desecration of the Temple) under Antiochus Epiphanes (167–164BCE) – contemporary with 1 and 2 Maccabees*. The first six chapters describe the life of Daniel, a Jewish exile at the court of Nebuchadnezzar (605–562BCE), and Daniel's faithfulness to the *Torah*. The stories of Daniel in the Furance and the Lions' Den illustrate this. The remainder of the book contains allegorical visions relating to the period of the persecution. The historical detail is confused, but the message is one of faithfulness to the traditions* of the Jewish people. It is from Daniel that the apocalyptic* term 'Son of Man' comes. The New Testament* used this title to refer to the suffering and glorified Christ*.

Hosea Hosea was a prophet* during the last years of the Northern Kingdom of Israel in the eighth century BCE, before its conquering by Assyria. He conceives the relationship between God* and the people as one like a marriage*. He himself seems to have married an unfaithful wife, Gomer. He saw his marital turmoil as a reflection of the unfaithfulness of Israel to God. He sees God as the faithful husband, and the qualities needed for fidelity by the people: justice, loyalty, compassion. Probable date for the present text of Hosea: 650BCE.

Joel The liturgical* quality of Joel suggests a connection with the Temple. He describes a plague of locusts and calls the people to repent and pray. The coming of the locusts is an image of the 'Day of the Lord', a day of fear and trembling, where nevertheless God* will triumph. From Joel comes the prophecy, used by Saint Peter* in Acts* 2:17–21 that God would 'pour out the Spirit* on all flesh'. Joel was probably composed in about 400BCE.

Amos Amos was a shepherd from Tekoa, near Jerusalem. He prophesied against the corruption, both religious* and political, of Israel in the period preceding its fall to the Assyrians in 721BCE, when his warning of the 'Day of the Lord' was fulfilled. The book was put together soon after the fall of the Kingdom.

Obadiah A short prophetic book on the theme of the coming 'Day of the Lord', probably composed some years after the destruction of Jerusalem in 586BCE; some of the text is also found in Jeremiah* (Jeremiah chapter 49).

Jonah This book, a work of fiction, is best described as a satire on human foibles which shows how merciful and compassionate God* is to everyone, whether Jewish or not. In speaking of the 'sign* of Jonah' (Matthew* 12:38–41, Luke* 11:29–32) Jesus* likens himself to Jonah, who preached* repentance* and spent three days in the belly of a fish – an allusion to Jesus' burial* and Resurrection*. The book is dated about 330BCE.

Micah A contemporary of Isaiah*, sharing Isaiah's hope* in a coming Messiah* of David's line. He mentions Bethlehem as the place of the Messiah's origins (5:1). The book is later than the material it contains, *c.*520BCE.

Nahum This is a short alphabetical poem on the fall of Nineveh in Assyria to the Babylonians and Medes, and must be close to the event in date (612BCE).

Habakkuk The book is in three parts; part 1 is a reflection on why wicked people triumph, part 2 is a series of curses on Babylon, the oppressor, and part 3 is a liturgical* hymn* celebrating the triumph of God. The book may be dated *c.*605–597BCE.

Zephaniah Zephaniah prophesied in the reign of Josiah (640–609BCE). He spoke of the coming 'Day of the Lord' which will purify Judah and its people. Those who remain after the disaster will form a humble, God-fearing 'remnant'.

Haggai Haggai was prophet* in the community that returned to Jerusalem after the exile, in 520BCE. His word was to encourage those rebuilding the Temple and ensure the purity of its worship*.

Zechariah This book is in two parts. Part 1 (chapters 1–8) is the prophecy of Zechariah, contemporary with Haggai* and in the same vein. It takes the form of eight symbolic visions and their interpretation. Part 2 (chapters 9–14) is perhaps 200 years later. It offers the hope of a royal Messiah* and a glorious future for Jerusalem in the last days. Part 1 may be dated *c.*520BCE, part 2 is from *c.*320BCE.

Malachi ('my messenger') This book consists of six passages about purity of religious* observance, written some years after the return from exile. To those who act and worship* corruptly, the 'Day of the Lord' will come as a purifying fire of judgement*. The date of Malachi is some time after the return from exile, *c.*450BCE.

The New Testament

The New Testament is Christian 'Scripture*'. It consists of four 'Gospels*' – affirmations of Jesus'* status as Son of God* and Christ* or Messiah. These are followed by the 'Acts of the Apostles'*, a book recounting the first apostolic* preaching* and concentrating on the missions* of Saint Paul*. Saint Paul's Letters*, together with other Letters, follow. These are sometimes known as 'Epistles' (Latin *epistola* – letter). The Apocalypse* (Greek *apocalypsis* – revelation) is the last book of the New Testament*.

The Gospels

The word 'gospel' is Old English for 'good news' (as in Greek *eu* – good and *angelion* – news). In the time after the apostles*, there were many accounts of the life of Jesus* claiming to be 'gospel'. In the second century, the Church* decided that the four which came under the names of Matthew* the Apostle, Mark*, Luke* and John* the Apostle should be accepted as 'canonical'*. Each claims to recount the mission* of Jesus, and all four climax in the account of his Passion* and Resurrection*.

Synoptic Gospels The first three Gospels, Matthew, Mark and Luke, are known as 'Synoptic' Gospels* (Greek *synopsis* – overview). They share a lot of subject matter and scholars are divided on how exactly they relate to one another and how they were sourced. Mark may be the oldest in its present form. Many scholars think that a document, now no longer existing, and known as 'Q'* (German *quellen* – source) may have provided a link between Matthew and Luke. It seems that Luke is the first part of a two-part account of the mission of Jesus and then of the apostles, in particular Saint Paul*. This forms our Book of the Acts of the Apostles*. Saint John's Gospel* is unlike the first three and has several unique features.

Matthew Saint Matthew's Gospel may have been intended for a Jewish audience. More use is made of the Old Testament* than in the other Gospels. He portrays Jesus as Son of David, Second Moses, Saviour* and teacher. The Gospel is built up around a collection of five 'sermons*' or collections of teaching, analogous to the five books of the Jewish *Torah*. These are: the Sermon on the Mount (chapters 5–7), missionary discourse (chapters 10–11), parables* (chapter 13), community sermon (chapter 18) and an apocalyptic* discourse (chapters 24–5). While it is an open question whether Matthew the Apostle* is the 'author' of this Gospel, its probable date is *c.*70CE.

Mark This is thought to be the earliest Gospel, written about 65–70CE. It concentrates on the person rather than the teaching of Jesus*. Its paradox is that Jesus is acknowledged as Son* of God*, both by the Father* and by the evil spirits, yet his own people reject him and the disciples* do not understand him. Its theme is the suffering of the Messiah*. Tradition* states that this Gospel reflects the teaching of Saint Peter*, whose affirmation of Jesus' divinity (8:29) acts as the watershed of the Gospel.

Luke Saint Luke was the companion of Saint Paul*, and this Gospel concentrates on Jesus* as the Saviour* of the Gentiles*. It portrays Jesus as the merciful and forgiving One. The poor, women and outcasts feature particularly in this Gospel. Some of the most famous of Jesus' parables*: the Samaritan, the Pharisee and the Tax Collector, the Prodigal Son, are found only in Luke. The Gospel is strong on personal morality and religious* practice. It seems to have been created for a Greek-speaking milieu about 80–5CE. It is probably the first part of a two-volume work, of which the Acts of the Apostles* is the second section.

John The fourth Gospel offers a different view of Jesus*. As a text it is more carefully wrought and material is arranged in the sequence of an event followed by discourse. Jesus is portrayed as the pre-existent Son* and Word* (*Logos**) of God*, and the revelation* of the Father*. He reveals his 'glory' through 'signs*' – works of power such as the changing of water* into wine* at Cana (2:1–11). His presence in the Church* is guaranteed through the Holy Spirit*. He replaces in his own person the Temple and religious* institutions of the Jews. People are judged by their response to him. Finally, the narrative of his Passion* reads like a triumphant affirmation of his divine Lordship and accomplishment. Tradition* suggests that the Gospel was written about 100CE, perhaps in Asia Minor.

Acts of the Apostles Acts records the story of the spread of the Christian* faith* from Judaea, through Asia Minor and eventually to Rome itself. It starts with the Ascension* of Jesus* and the gift of the Spirit* at Pentecost*, continuing with an account of the preaching* of Peter* and then of the journeys of Paul*. Parts of Saint Paul's journeys are described in the first person, suggesting that the writer (usually regarded as Saint Luke) was Saint Paul's travelling companion. Acts shows some of the issues that confronted the Church*: the admission of Gentile* Christians, relationships with the Roman state and with pagan* religious* practice. The book was probably separated from the Gospel of Saint Luke* when the canon* of Christian Scripture* was formed in *c.*150CE.

The Letters

Letters of Saint Paul

Saint Paul* seems to have been a prolific writer, using letters to the communities that he founded or visited to continue his teaching among them. He used letters to answer questions about faith* and conduct, to lay down lines of teaching about Jesus*, and to instil discipline in the communities to which he wrote. In the New Testament*, the letters are usually printed in order of length, but this is not their chronological order. This might be as follows: the early letters: 1 and 2 Thessalonians*; the major dogmatic* letters: 1 and 2 Corinthians*, Galatians*, Romans*, possibly Philippians*; the letters written from prison: Colossians*, Ephesians*, Philemon*; the 'Pastoral' letters*: 1 and 2 Timothy*, Titus*. Paul's authorship of some of these later letters is disputed.

The Letter to the Hebrews* is not usually regarded as being by Saint Paul.

Romans This, the longest of Saint Paul's* letters, is probably his personal introduction to the Church* of Rome, a mixed community of Jewish and Gentile* Christians* whom he proposed to visit. It is a major dogmatic* treatise about the relationship between Judaism and Christianity. Saint Paul argues that only God's* gift of faith* in Christ* can bring salvation*. The Jewish Law is ineffective and can only give knowledge of sin*. Faith is ritualised in baptism*, by which we die with Christ to rise with him to a new life, given vitality and substance by the Holy Spirit*. The second part of the letter is a reflection on the destiny of the Jewish people. Romans was probably written *c.*57CE from Corinth.

1 Corinthians Corinth, a port, had a lively Christian* community. Paul* is addressing difficulties in the community and answering questions brought to him by their elders. In this, Paul teaches about Christ* as God's Wisdom, the Church* as Christ's body* – including the first explicit mention (10:15–17,

11:23–7) of the Eucharist* – and the gifts of the Spirit* that give life to the Church. He stresses the importance of interpreting and regulating these gifts. Finally, he writes movingly of the Resurrection* of Christ as the archetype of Christian resurrection. This letter was written from Ephesus, c.54CE.

2 Corinthians This is possibly a collection of letters, with chapters 1–9 being written from Macedonia and 10–13 from Ephesus, c.55–6CE. It represents a further attempt by Paul* to bring order to the fractious community. He reflects on his integrity as an apostle* and commends a collection for the Jerusalem Church* as a means to unity*. The final section is autobiographical.

Galatians Paul* is writing to a community tempted to make the Jewish Law obligatory on Christians*. His purpose is to show that the Cross* of Christ* sets aside the Law and that the true children of Abraham are those who have faith*. He recounts his conversion* and meeting with Peter*, and the authenticity of his mission* to Gentiles*. He calls for a recognition of the fruits of the Spirit* as the basis of Christian conduct. Galatians was probably written c.56CE.

Ephesians This letter celebrates Christ* as the Lord* of the Cosmos, the fullness of creation, the new Adam*, and portrays the Church* as Christ's body*, his completion, filled with divine life. The letter expounds the 'mystery*' of Christ now revealed to believers. The style is elaborate and liturgical* and closely related to Paul's* letter to the Colossians*. Paul's authorship of Ephesians is disputed, but there is no doubt as to its theological importance and the Pauline nature of its teaching. It seems to have been written c.60CE, possibly from Rome.

Philippians This is a joyful letter expressing great affection for the Philippi Christian* community. It incorporates an early hymn* about Christ* the Servant of God* (2:6–11) and the famous exhortation to 'Rejoice!' (4:4–8). This letter may in fact be a collection of short texts (a suggested breakdown is 1:1–3 and 4:2–9; 4:10–20; 3:2–4:1) and its date is uncertain, perhaps c.56CE.

Colossians This letter seems to have been written to counteract the desire of the Jewish Christians* of Colossae to worship angels* and cosmic powers. Paul* insists that Christ* is above all these and is the true image of God*, God's Wisdom, in whom the fullness of divinity exists. Paul reflects on membership of Christ's body* and the sufferings that accompany it. The letter was written from Rome, c.60CE.

1 Thessalonians This is probably the earliest of Saint Paul's* letters, written after a visit to the Thessalonica community. He thanks them for their patience and faith* and comments on the recent visit of his pupil Timothy to them. The letter is important in that it reflects Saint Paul's early understanding of Christ's* imminent return, which he describes in the language of Jewish apocalypse*. The letter may be dated c.50CE, written from Corinth.

2 Thessalonians This is a follow-up to the previous letter and looks like an attempt to calm speculation about Christ's* imminent return. Saint Paul* encourages patience and firmness in faith*, and writes against disunity and idleness. Probable date: c.51CE and written in Corinth.

The Pastoral Letters

These letters claim to be addressed to men whom Saint Paul* had put in charge of Christian* communities. They concern pastoral* care and the development of their communities as these move into their second generation and develop in a Hellenistic environment. Though they may quote liturgical* texts (1 Timothy* 3:16), these letters are more manuals of instruction for pastors* than treatises on doctrine*. It is not easy to fit these letters into Saint Paul's style or interests. They may be attributed to him as a means of giving them authority – a practice common in the ancient world. The dating of these letters is uncertain.

1 Timothy This letter contains warnings against false teaching and instructions concerning prayer*, women in the community, widows*, elders and slaves.

2 Timothy A personal letter, asking Timothy to be mindful of his calling and the gifts he has received in ordination*. It warns him of the hardships he must face, the dangers of false teaching and the need to live an upright life.

Titus This letter contains instructions on the choice and appointment of elders, the dangers of false teaching and the need to model Christian* behaviour on Christ's* sacrifice*, ritualised for Christians in baptism*.

Philemon This is a personal appeal to a friend (and convert) to take back Onesimus, a slave who had absconded. Saint Paul* urges Philemon to receive Onesimus not only as a slave but as a brother in Christ*. The letter was written from Rome, c.60CE.

Hebrews This anonymous letter, attached to Saint Paul's* writings, was written to a group of Jews, possibly Temple staff, who as Christian* converts missed the ritual* and splendour of Temple worship*. It uses Scripture* to show that Christ's* death* was a once-for-all sacrifice* which formed a new covenant* to fulfil all God's* promises and the rituals of old. It is an important letter, because it outlines a theology* of the eternal priesthood* of Christ, which forms a powerful set of liturgical* images. The author interprets the journey of the Israelites in the desert after the Exodus* from Egypt as a foretelling of the Christian journey to the final place of rest, and offers the faith* of the patriarchs* as a model for Christian hope*. The letter was probably written around the time of the destruction of the Temple, 70CE.

The Letters to all Christians

The seven letters that end the epistle* section of the New Testament* are addressed to all Christians*. For that reason they are known as the 'Catholic* Epistles'. They are attributed to various of the apostles* and reflect a world where Christians were having to come to terms with the pagan* world.

James This is a letter addressed particularly to Christians* of Jewish origin scattered throughout the Roman Empire. It is practical and concerned with faith* expressing itself in good works. It particularly commends the anointing* of the sick as a ritual* of healing* and forgiveness. Its date is disputed, some scholars making it the earliest New Testament* document and others placing it at the end of the first century CE. Its attribution to James the 'brother of the Lord*' and head of the Jerusalem Church* is also disputed.

1 Peter A letter to Christians* in Asia Minor who were suffering persecution. The letter employs the theme of baptism* as a source of new life, so it is probable that it was written to new converts. The themes of suffering with Christ* and the practicalities of Christian living are also present in the letter.

The letter has always been accepted as authentic, from Peter's* preaching* (if not his hand) and written some time before 67CE, from Rome.

2 Peter This second letter, almost certainly not from Peter* himself, encourages readers to await the Day of the Lord* Jesus* with patience and perseverance. It warns against false teachers. Parts of it are similar to the Letter of Jude* (2:1–3:3). It may be dated after 90CE.

1 John The three letters of John are like the Gospel of John* in style, so they are thought to be authentic. The first letter dwells on two of John's characteristic ideas: that Christ* is the Light*, the revelation* of the Father*, and that the Christian's* life must be on the side of light against darkness, and centre on the two commandments* of love of God* and neighbour. It warns its readers to guard against the 'Antichrist' – probably a group within the community who had separated themselves from it. The letter was probably written *c.*100CE.

2 John A footnote to the first letter, as an argument against those who denied the reality of the Incarnation*. Date: probably *c.*100CE.

3 John A letter dealing with a dissident church* member who was causing division in the community, dated *c.*100CE.

Jude The author claims to be Jude, a brother of the Lord*. The letter uses Old Testament* and Jewish apocalyptic* imagery to warn against false teachers and encourage reliance on the mercy of Christ*. Jude is a probable partial source of 2 Peter*. Probable date: *c.*90CE.

The Apocalypse (Revelation) This is a Christian* apocalypse*, drawing heavily on Jewish apocalyptic* material such as that found in the Books of Ezekiel* and Daniel*. Written as an encouragement to persevere under harsh persecution, it portrays the struggle as a cosmic and final one between the chosen of God* and the evil that seeks to destroy them. The book begins with addresses to the 'Seven Churches of Asia' and continues in four prophetic visions to describe the prelude to the Day of God (chapters 4–16), the punishment of Rome, portrayed as 'Babylon' (17:1–19:10), the destruction of unbelievers (19:11–20:15) and the heavenly Jerusalem (chapters 21, 22) where God lives among mortals. The images are memorable: the four beasts (4:4–8), the seven seals (chapters 5, 6), the trumpets (8:6–9:21), the woman and the dragon (chapter 12), the triumph of the Lamb (chapter 14), the seven bowls of plagues (15:5–16:21). The text takes up themes found in Saint John's Gospel* such as that of the victorious Lamb. Though ascribed to John* and similar in some ways to his Gospel, the text is more probably from his circle. It may be dated to 68CE (the persecution by Emperor Nero) or, more likely, to 95CE (the persecution by Emperor Domitian).

MINISTRY

Explanation

This section deals with ministry in the Church*. The whole Church is a community called to ministry – service of the world under the guidance of the gospel*. From the time of the New Testament*, the Church has understood itself as a body* composed of many different people with gifts* that differ. All these gifts may be used for the service or ministry of the whole body. Within the Church, many individuals exercise ministry to the Church community.

Some of these individuals are ordained* – they have a specific identity and exercise specific leadership roles in worship* and pastoral* care. These are summarised below (see **Orders and Ordination**). Others also, though not ordained, exercise liturgical* and pastoral functions (see **Non-ordained ministries**).

Orders and Ordination (Latin *ordo* – an 'order' or functioning group of people)

The Catholic* Church* has three orders, that of bishop*, priest* and deacon*. Of these the bishop is the most important. Even the Pope* is, in terms of ordination, simply a bishop. The Church regards bishops as the successors of Christ's* Apostles* acting in communion* with the Pope, the successor of Peter*. Acting in the name of Christ*, bishops have a three-fold ministry of teaching, sanctifying and ruling the communities or dioceses* over which they preside. Bishops have priests as their co-workers in the task of teaching, making holy* and ruling their diocese. Bishops also have deacons to assist them and their priests.

To be ordained*, one must be a baptised and confirmed believer who has a vocation*, i.e., a formal calling from the Church to be ordained. This formal calling confirms the personal conviction of the ordinand*. Ordination is a sacrament* and can only be celebrated by the bishop. One must be at least 23 years old to be ordained deacon (35 if married), 25 to be ordained priest and at least 35 to be ordained bishop.

Ministry of the Deacon (Greek *diaconos* – servant)
Deacons are of two types, those proceeding to be ordained* priest* and permanent deacons, who may be married.

A deacon can:
(a) lead the Liturgy of the Hours* and liturgies of the Word*

113

(b) proclaim the Gospel* at Mass*
(c) preach* the homily*
(d) administer Holy Communion*
(e) baptise*
(f) officiate at marriages*
(g) conduct funerals*
(h) exercise a pastoral* ministry*.
A deacon cannot:
(a) celebrate Mass
(b) confirm
(c) ordain*
(d) give absolution* in the Sacrament of Penance*.

Ministry of the Priest (Greek *presbyteros* – elder)
A priest can:
(a) do all that a deacon* does, and:
(b) celebrate Mass*
(c) give absolution* in the Sacrament of Penance*.
A priest cannot:
(a) confirm
(b) ordain*.

Ministry of the Bishop (Greek *episcopos* – overseer)
The term 'bishop' is an Anglo-Saxon version of the Latin *episcopus*.
A bishop can:
(a) do all that a deacon* does
(b) do all that a priest* does
and
(c) confirm
(d) ordain*.
In this way the bishop:
(a) has the 'fullness' of ministry*
(b) is the source of ministry.

Non-ordained Ministries

In addition to ministries for which ordination* is required, the Church* has ministries open to those not ordained* such as acolyte*, extraordinary minister of communion* and reader*.

Ministry and governance For all other entries relating to the roles exercised by the ordained* and others in the government of the Church*, see the section 'Organisation and Governance', page 143.

Word List

Acolyte The acolyte assists the priest* or deacon* at services*. At Mass*, acolytes will carry the candles* and incense*, help prepare the altar* at the preparation of the gifts and distribute Holy Communion*. Admission to this ministry* is obligatory for all who are training for ordination*. Acolytes are admitted to their ministry by the bishop* or major religious* superior*. Lay* people can also act as acolytes.

Bishop (Greek *episcopos* – overseer) The chief minister* of the Church* in a diocese*. The bishop is seen as the successor of Christ's* apostles* and of the High Priest. See **Orders and Ordination** above.

Cantor (Latin *cantare* – to sing) The minister* who leads the singing at worship*. According to the Roman Missal* of 1970, the cantor is a required minister* at every Mass*.

Deacon (Greek *diaconos* – servant) The minister* ordained* for the service of worship* and charity* – the administration of the Church's* charitable work. See **Orders and Ordination** above.

Diaconate (Greek *diaconos* – servant) The office of deacon*.

Episcopate (Greek *episcopos* – overseer) The office of bishop*, also the time that a bishop spends in office.

Extraordinary minister of communion Where there are not enough priests*, deacons* or acolytes* to give communion*, lay* people are encouraged to assist. They will also take the Blessed Sacrament* to the sick. Some training is obligatory though a priest can, on occasion, depute a member of the congregation* to act as a communion minister*. Extraordinary ministers are admitted to ministry by the bishop*, dean* or parish priest*.

Lay (Greek *laos* – the people) The generic term for all the members of the Church*, the people of God*. However, it is usually used to denote those who are not ordained*.

Lay ministries (Latin *ministerium* – service) Lay* people, both men and women, also exercise a ministry* at Mass* and other services* as readers*, servers*, cantors* and in other ways.

Lector (Latin *legere* – to read) A minister* charged with reading the Scriptures* at the liturgy*. The role of lector may be taken by lay men or women.

Minister (Latin *ministerium* – service) The title given to anyone who serves the Church* community in worship* or pastoral* care.

Ministry (Latin *ministerium* – service) The collective term for all ministers*, and the state of being a minister.

Ordain (Latin *ordinare* – to allot an order) To create a bishop*, priest* or deacon* by the ritual* action of imposition of hands* by the bishop* and the prayer* of ordination*.

Ordinand (Latin *ordinare* – to allot an order) One who is to be ordained* to ministry*.

Ordination (Latin *ordinatio* – allotting an order) The act of creating a bishop*, priest* or deacon* by the laying on of hands* and prayer*.

Pontifical (Latin *pontifex* – bridge-builder) The state of being a bishop*.

Presbyter (Greek *presbuteros* – elder) A priest*. The term is little used, since the usual English version of the term is 'priest'.

Presbyterate (Greek *presbuteros* – elder) The priesthood*, the state of being a priest*. The term is also used as a collective to describe the priests of a diocese*.

Priest (Greek *presbuteros* – elder) One ordained* to the ministry* of priesthood*. See **Orders and Ordination** above.

Priesthood (Latin *presbyteratus* – priesthood) The state of being a priest*.

Reader The reader proclaims the Scripture* readings at Mass*, and may also act as a catechist*. Readers are formally admitted to ministry* by the bishop* or major religious* superior*. Reception of this ministry* is obligatory for all who are training for ordination*. Lay* people can also act as readers.

Subdeacon The order* of ministry* formerly below that of deacon.* The subdeacon assisted the deacon* and priest* at High Mass*. He was responsible for the care of the altar cloths* and other linen used at Mass*. The office of subdeacon was abolished in 1970.

Vocation (Latin *vocare* – to call) The moment in the Ordination* Rite* when the bishop* formally calls the candidate forward and seeks the assent of the people for him to be ordained*. The term is also used to refer to the sense that a person may have that they are called to ministry* in the Church*.

DRESS OF MINISTERS

A priest in Mass vestments

Alb (Latin *albus* – white) The white robe, with long sleeves, covering the body from neck to ankle, which is worn by all ministers* for Mass* and other services*. It may be worn with an amice* at the neck and a cincture* to hold it round the middle. It is descended from the Roman linen tunic that was worn under civilian dress. In the medieval period it symbolised purity.

Amice (Latin *amictus* – garment) A rectangle of linen worn to cover the neck and secured with tapes crossed around the body. It is worn with the alb*. In medieval symbolism it represented the 'helmet of salvation'.

Apparel A strip of precious fabric or embroidery sometimes attached to the upper edge of the amice* and thrown back over the outer vestment* to form a sort of collar. Albs* can also have apparels, usually on the cuffs and the lower front and back hem.

Biretta The square cap, adorned with wings and a tassel, sometimes worn by ordained* ministers.

Cappa magna (Latin for 'great cloak') The ceremonial dress (not worn when celebrating Mass*) of the bishop*, consisting of a large caped cloak with a long train, usually made of silk, purple for a bishop and red for a cardinal*.

Cassock (Old French *casaque* – a long coat) The robe often worn by clergy* under the vestments*. It is a long-sleeved coat done up with buttons down the middle and worn with a cincture*. Priests* wear black cassocks. For formal occasions, bishops* wear purple, and cardinals* red, cassocks. On other occasions the cassock is black, but the cincture and trimmings are purple or red.

Chasuble The outermost vestment* worn at Mass*. Traditionally, it took the form of a conical tent-shaped garment with a hole for the head. In the Middle Ages when it came to be made of precious fabrics or embroidered cloth, it was progressively cut away at the sides to resemble little more than a sort of sandwich-board. Modern practice has restored something of the more ample shape. In colour, the chasuble will follow the liturgical colour* of the season* or feast*. Medieval symbolism thought of it as representing the 'gentle yoke' of Christ*.

Cincture (Latin *cingere* – to gird) The rope that may hold the alb* in at the waist. The term is also used of the wide cloth or silk band worn at the waist with the cassock*. This is purple for bishops* and red for cardinals*.

Choir dress The robes worn over the cassock* by the priest* or bishop* when not celebrating Mass* or presiding at a liturgical* service*. Usually choir dress* is the surplice* or cotta* with a mozzetta* or mantelletta* for more senior priests.

Cloak The long loose cloak, usually black, worn as a protection against cold when taking services* outdoors.

Cope (Latin *cappa* – cloak) A large semicircular cloak worn by priests* for certain liturgical* services* and processions*, when not wearing the chasuble*. The cope may also worn by lay* people such as cantors*. It is often richly decorated and has a hood, now often simply a flat semicircular flap attached to the centre of the neck.

Cotta (Italian for 'shortened') A version of the surplice* but with tighter sleeves and square neck, formal pleats and reaching to the knee.

Crosier (Medieval Latin *crocia*) The staff carried by the bishop*, or by the abbot* or abbess* of a monastery* as a sign* of their pastoral* oversight. It is held during services*, especially when giving blessings*. In shape it is a straight staff with curved or crook-shaped head.

Dalmatic The distinctive vestment of the deacon*, worn over the alb* and stole*. It is a tunic with sleeves, reaching to the knees or ankles and often adorned with two vertical stripes called *clavi*, running front to back over the shoulders.

Girdle See **Cincture**

Hood Sometimes a hood is worn with the alb* instead of the amice*, particularly by members of some religious* orders*. A small hood is also part of the mozzetta*.

Humeral veil (Latin *humerale* – of the shoulder) The long rectangular veil worn

A deacon vested for Mass

at Benediction* when the Blessed Sacrament* is carried in the monstrance*. The monstrance is held through the veil.

Maniple (Latin *manipulum* – a handkerchief) The vestment formerly worn by ordained* ministers* at Mass*. It was a strip of cloth, in colour and decoration like the stole*, worn over the left wrist. Medieval·tradition* interpreted it as a sign of earthly suffering, endured in hope* of heavenly reward.

Mantelletta (Italian – small cloak) The sleeveless coat, open at the front, worn by some senior priests*, particularly members of the Roman Curia* and monsignors*. Its colour reflects the rank of the wearer.

Mitre (Greek *mitra* – a turban) The pointed headdress worn by bishops* and

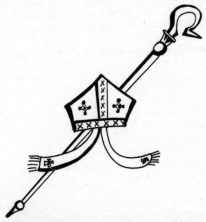

The mitre and pastoral staff of a bishop

119

abbots*. The mitre is usually white or gold and does not follow the colour of the liturgical* season*. For funerals*, and other solemn occasions, it is of plain white linen.

Mozzetta (Italian) A short cape worn by canons* of cathedrals* and other priests*, with a hood* attached.

Orphrey (Latin *aurifrigium* – gold embroidery) The ornamental bands found on vestments*, particularly the chasuble*, dalmatic* and cope*, and on altar* frontals*. The orphrey was formerly made of precious material.

Pastoral staff The staff carried in the liturgy* by the bishop*. It is often shaped in the form of a shepherd's crook.

Pectoral cross (Latin *pectus* – breast) The cross* worn by the bishop* or by the abbot* or abbess* of a monastery* on the breast, suspended by a neck chain or silken cord. It originally contained relics*.

Ring The ring is worn by the bishop* or by the abbot* or abbess* of a monastery* on the third finger of the right hand. It is a very ancient ornament, being mentioned as early as the seventh century. Rings are also worn by female religious*. The ring symbolises marriage* to the Church*.

Rochet (German *rock* – a coat) A garment like the cotta*, with closer sleeves, worn by some senior priests* as choir dress*.

Stole (Greek *stole* – robe) A narrow band of cloth, usually of the same material as the chasuble* or cope*, worn underneath these vestments* at Mass* and other services*. It may also be worn at other times. Bishops* and priests* wear the stole round the neck and hanging down in front. The deacon* wears it over the left shoulder, tied at the right hip. Medieval symbolism made it represent the robe of immortality.

Surplice (Latin *super pelliceum* – over a fur coat) A version of the alb* developed for use in cold medieval churches* to be worn over a thick fur cassock*. The surplice is much looser than the alb* and the sleeves are wider. The priest* wears the surplice at liturgical* services* when not wearing the alb. The surplice may be worn by all ministers*. See also **Cotta**

Tunicle (Latin *tunicula* – tunic) Formerly the vestment* of the subdeacon*, resembling the dalmatic*, only slightly shorter and plainer.

Vestments (Latin *vestimentum* – clothing) The common term for all the liturgical* garments of the Church*.

Zucchetto (Italian) The small skullcap worn by bishops* (purple) and cardinals* (red).

THE RELIGIOUS LIFE

Within the Church* are individuals and communities who follow a distinctive lifestyle. Most live more or less in community and all follow some sort of rule* of life. They are known collectively as *religious*.

In New Testament* times, there were special groups, such as widows*, recognised by the Church with defined prayer* and pastoral* roles. We know too that many people living alone undertook sustained prayer and ascesis*. However, it was in Egypt during the third century CE that recognisable religious life began. These beginnings are associated with Saint* Antony (*c.*251–356CE), a hermit* of the Egyptian desert, who gathered round him a community of disciples*, and Saint Pachomius (*c.*290–356CE), who founded communities in the desert.

This new community life spread rapidly first to Palestine and then to southern France and Ireland. Groups of monks* living in an enclosure* met together for prayer at regular intervals, day and night. Their prayer was based on the continuous recitation of the Psalms* and they undertook simple, repetitive work such as basket-making or agriculture.

Later communities diversified both the prayer and the work. In the sixth century CE, Saint Benedict produced the *Rule for Monks** (probably at his monastery* of Monte Cassino) to legislate for his new communities in Italy. This became the most popular monastic rule in the Churches of Europe and the Benedictine* system gave rise to great monastic centres of culture in the eighth, ninth and tenth centuries CE and since.

In the eleventh and twelfth centuries a major reform of the Benedictine tradition resulted in the formation of the Cistercian* Order* – a more austere way of keeping the Rule. A little later, a new type of religious community emerged: the Friars*, beginning with the Dominicans* and Franciscans* in southern France and Italy. These friars were able to live on the move as well as in settled communities, and worked as teachers and preachers* of the faith*. In the sixteenth century there arose a new style of religious life typified by the Jesuits*, founded as an order taking its mission* directly from the Pope*. In the seventeenth century, and again in the years after the French Revolution, new communities were founded to cope with the education and care of the poor, and later still for missionary* work in the new colonial empires of the nineteenth century.

Religious life is always evolving, and over the last forty years, groups known as 'new movements' have emerged that are not always community based but are formed of men and women living independently who keep a common rule of life and assemble regularly together. Some of the better known of these are included in the word list.

THE SANCTIFYING CHURCH

There are some hundreds of religious orders in the Church. It would not be possible to account for them all. This section will list the principal groupings into which most communities fit. Broadly speaking, religious can be divided into those who live in monasteries with little or no formal pastoral involvement outside, and those who, though they live in communities, are fully engaged with pastoral work of various kinds. Also, the major groupings are usually associated with the name of the founder or inspirer.

Abbess (Syriac *abba* – father, Latin *abbatissa*) The head of an abbey* of women, elected by the community and entrusted with its governance. The abbess uses the crosier* and ring* as insignia of office.

Abbey A community of monks* or nuns* governed by an abbot* or abbess*. An abbey usually comprises twelve or more fully professed members. The term is also applied to the church* building used by such a community.

Abbot (Syriac *abba* – father, Latin *abbas*) The head of an abbey* of men, elected by the community and entrusted with its governance. The abbot uses the insignia of a bishop: the crosier*, mitre* and ring*.

Ascesis/ticism (Greek *askesis* – self-denial) The practice of fasting and other disciplines associated with many saints* and founders of religious* orders*.

Augustinians A large grouping of communities, monastic*, apostolic* and missionary*, who follow a rule* associated with Saint* Augustine of Hippo (354–430CE). Augustine established a community at Thagaste in 388CE and groups bearing his name (Augustinian or Austin) flourished throughout the Middle Ages. A major reform took place in the late sixteenth century. Members may be ordained* or lay*.

Benedictines Saint* Benedict (480–550CE) wrote the *Rule** which regulates Benedictine monasteries*. There are monasteries both of monks* and nuns*. Each monastery is an independent community, ruled by its abbot* or abbess*, but monasteries are grouped nowadays into 'congregations*' which have similar observances and regulate each other. The habit* of Benedictines is usually black, a long belted tunic worn with a veil* for women and hood* for men, and a scapular*. Benedictines assemble several times each day for the Liturgy of the Hours* and for Mass*. Benedictines may be ordained* or lay*.

Brothers In the Middle Ages, monasteries* had 'lay* brothers' – men not ordained* who served the monastery in practical tasks. The Franciscans* and Dominicans* had them also. Also, communities of laymen were formed to work among the poor, lepers, and victims of war. After the Council of Trent* and in the nineteenth century, orders* of brothers became active in education, which is still their major function.

Calefactory (Latin *calor* – heat, and *facere* – to make) The name for the recreation or common room in some monasteries*.

Canons regular Groups of male and female religious* who, though not monks*, live and pray in community. Canons emerged in the early Middle Ages as groups of priests* attached to cathedrals* and great churches*. Later, as attempts were made to improve the life of priests, the community life was taken up by other groups of clergy*. The main groups of Canons and Canonesses regular today engage in parish* and educational work.

Carmelites The Carmelites trace their ancestry to hermits* living on Mount Carmel in Palestine, claiming spiritual descent from the Prophet* Elijah. Their traditions* came to western Europe with returning Crusaders. They became organised as communities of friars*. Communities of women also formed. In the sixteenth century there was a major reform associated with Saint* Teresa of Avila (1515–82) who formed enclosed* female Carmelite communities. Carmelites engage in pastoral*, missionary* and educative work. The habit* is brown, with a white cloak* worn in church*.

Carthusians In the eleventh century Saint* Bruno (c.1032–1101), the Chancellor of Rheims Cathedral*, experienced a calling to life as a hermit*. He gathered a band of disciples* and founded La Grande Chartreuse, in the remote country near Grenoble, in 1084. Houses of the order* were established elsewhere. The Carthusians are organised into communities, each under a prior*. The community is divided into priests*, who live as solitaries, and lay*, brothers* who live in community, serve the priests and manage the monastery*. They have no external involvement. The habit* is white with a tunic and hood*. The scapular* has two broad bands of cloth joining the back and front flaps.

Cell (Latin *cella* – chamber) The living quarters of monks* and nuns*. The first monks and nuns lived in small huts grouped round the church*. Saint* Benedict envisaged everyone sleeping in a common dormitory, and this new arrangement reflected the growing community life expressed in the Middle Ages in the great monastic complexes where church* and living quarters formed part of one single establishment. After the sixteenth century, communities returned to the practice of each monk or nun occupying a single cell. Carthusians* live in cells built like tiny two-storey cottages.

Chapter (Latin *capitulum* – heading or chapter) A formal meeting of religious*. Some orders* have a general chapter which brings together representatives of the whole order.

Chapter house (Latin *capitulum* – heading or chapter) The meeting and business place of the monastery*, named after the 'chapter' or short Scripture* reading that opened all meetings there. The chapter house usually occupies the eastern side of the cloister*.

Cistercians (from the Abbey of Citeaux) At the end of the eleventh century, there was a reform movement within the Benedictine* Order, associated particularly with the name of Saint* Bernard of Clairvaux (1090–1153). The reformers wanted a more austere observance of the rule* and less involvement with secular politics and society. The first monasteries* were established in France (Citeaux, Clairvaux) and the characteristic traits of the Cistercian reform codified in 1119. Cistercians chose locations for their monasteries in remote areas and specialised in farming. There exist both male and female Cistercian communities. The habit* is white, and similar to that of Benedictines*.

Cloister (Latin *clausura* – enclosure) In traditionally planned monasteries*, usually a square garden south of the church*, with a closed walkway around it, from which access is gained to all the principal rooms of the monastery. Medieval monks* used the cloister as a place for work and study.

Congregation (Latin *con* – with, and *grex* – flock) The name given to a group of religious* within a larger community. Benedictine* monks* are divided into congregations, which serve as administrative and organising units for visitations and other contact between monasteries*.

Convent (Latin *convenire* – to come together) The term for a monastic* community. The word is now used more loosely of any community of female religious*.

Conventual Of or pertaining to a monastery*.

Cursillo Movement (Spanish for 'a little course') A new religious* movement, founded in Spain in 1949. Cursillo works through intense three-day programmes of Christian* renewal, doctrinal*, spiritual* and liturgical*, with follow-up sessions.

Dame (Latin *domina* – mistress) The old English title for a fully professed Benedictine* nun*.

Dom (Latin *dominus* – master) The old English title for a fully professed Benedictine* monk*.

Dominicans (The Order* of Preachers*) The founder, Saint* Dominic (1170–1221) was an Augustinian* canon* of Osma Cathedral* in Spain. In 1203 he went to Provence, to preach against the Albigensian heresy*, a religious* movement imported from the East, which denied the Incarnation* and the goodness of the material creation. In 1206 he founded a convent* for nuns*, converts from Albigensianism, then went on to found other houses for men also. The community became known as the Order of Preachers. The order's statutes were approved in Rome in 1216. The Dominicans were renowned for their teaching in the new universities, a particularly famous member of the order being Saint Thomas Aquinas*. The Dominican Order consists of priests*, brothers* and sisters*. Dominican communities – both of men and women – engage in preaching, study, writing, teaching and work for justice and peace. The habit* is a white tunic (with veil* or hood*) and scapular* with black cloak* for use in church*.

Enclosure (Latin *clausura* – an enclosure) The space of a monastery* restricted to the monks* or nuns*. The term is also used to describe the state of female Benedictine* and other religious* who live lives totally within the enclosure and whose business with the outside world is conducted through lay* sisters*.

Focolare Movement (Italian for 'hearth') Founded by Silvia (Chiara) Lubich in the Italian city of Trent during the Second World War, the Focolare Movement is a way of following the Gospel* open to both unmarried and married people. Members either live in community if unmarried, or as families if married. The aim of Focolare is to practise the teaching of the Gospel, with its emphasis on mutual love and a particular interest in the unity* both of Christians* and of all humankind. Focolare is established worldwide, both within and outside the Catholic* Church*.

Franciscans (Order* of Friars* Minor/Order of Friars Minor Conventual/Order of Friars Minor Capuchin) The Franciscan 'family' of communities originates with the calling of Saint* Francis of Assisi (1181–1226). As a wealthy young man, Francis forsook his wealth and family to live the life of a beggar, and follow the gospel* teachings literally. Companions joined him, and eventually he founded the Order of Friars Minor in 1209 as a community of men observing poverty, common prayer*, preaching* and work among the poor. The order grew rapidly. Ten years after its foundation five thousand friars attended the first general chapter*. Francis himself was disappointed at the quarrels that later divided his brothers*, and retired to live as a hermit*, receiving the mystical experience of the stigmata* in 1224. The later history of the order has diversified the original community into the three principal groups referred to above. Medieval Franciscans were famous as teachers in the universities as well as preachers and pastors*. Today, within the three Franciscan traditions, both male and female

Franciscan communities exist. They work in parishes*, universities and schools and still exercise their calling to work among the poorest and marginalised. The habit* is usually brown, worn with cape and hood*.

Friar (Latin *frater* – brother and French *frere*) A male member of the Franciscan*, Dominican* or other group of religious*. Friars may be either ordained* or lay*.

Friars Minor The general term for Franciscans*. There are three varieties of Friars Minor: Friars Minor, Friars Minor Conventual and Friars Minor Capuchin.

Friary (Latin *frater* – brother and French *frere*) A building where friars* live in community.

General chapter (Latin *capitulum* – heading or chapter) The highest assembly of a religious order*.

Grail, the A community largely of lay* people, some living in community and others living as family members outside, founded in Holland by Father James Van Ginneken SJ in 1921. The Grail now exists as a worldwide organisation, with the aim of developing the faith of its members and contributing to the mission of the Church*.

Habit (Latin *habitus* – appearance, dress) The distinctive dress of monks*, nuns and other religious*.

Jesuits (Society of Jesus*) The largest religious* order* in the Church*, founded by Saint* Ignatius of Loyola (1491–1556) in 1540. After a military career, Ignatius was wounded and while recovering experienced a religious conversion*. He gathered a group of companions and started an apostolate* of missionary* and other work, with the ideal that the members of the Society should be directly at the disposal of the Pope*. In the troubled times of the sixteenth century the Jesuits were highly influential in strengthening and renewing the Catholic* Church* in Europe and ensuring conformity to the decrees of the Council of Trent*. Elsewhere, Jesuits took the mission* of the Church into the newly discovered territories of Latin America, and were among the first Europeans to live and work in India, China and Japan. Jesuits engage in pastoral*, educational and other work of many kinds. The Society contains priests* and brothers* as members.

Monastery (Greek *monazon* – one living a solitary life) Paradoxically, an abbey*, priory* or other community of monks* or nuns*.

Monk (Latin *monachus*) A male religious*, lay* or ordained*, following the Rule of Saint Benedict* or other monastic rule*.

Mercy, Sisters of One of the largest women's religious* orders*, this group of communities was founded by Catherine McAuley in 1831. They are dedicated to education, hospitals and care for the destitute.

Military orders Groups of knights founded at the time of the Crusades to defend the Christian kingdom of Jerusalem. Mostly now defunct, two main orders survive. See **Knights of Malta** and **Knights of the Holy Sepulchre**

Missionary congregations Many religious* orders* were formed to work in areas which were opened up by the colonial powers of the nineteenth century, particularly in Africa. Some were completely new foundations, others contained elements of the traditions* of older orders.

Neo-Catechumenate Movement (Greek *katechein* – to instruct) Properly known as the 'Neo-Catechumenal Way,' the movement was begun in 1962 by Kiko Arguello and Carmen Hernandez, who worked as evangelists* in the slums of Madrid. The movement spread to Rome in 1968. The movement aims to help people to reactivate their faith* and make real the calling received in baptism* to follow Christ*. Members work within parishes* as small communities, inviting people to take part in a post-baptismal catechumenate* leading to a renewal of baptismal promises and of their Christian* life.

Novice (Latin *novus* – new) A person received into an order* in a period of testing of vocation* and of training, but not yet fully professed.

Novitiate (Latin *novus* – new) Either the state of being a novice* or the part of the monastery* where the novices live somewhat apart from the professed monks*

Nun (Latin *nonna*, fem. of *nonnus* – in the Rule of Saint Benedict*, the term of address to a monk*) A female religious* living under the Rule of Saint Benedict or other monastic rule*.

Nunnery General term for any community of female religious*.

Oblates (Latin *oblatus* – someone given or offered) The title given to a number of religious* orders*, whose apostolate* is generally pastoral*, missionary* or educational. Oblates are also found within the Benedictine* tradition*, as men and women who, though not living a monastic life, wish to be associated with its aims. Most monasteries* appoint one of their monks* or nuns* as the director of oblates.

Opus Dei An international organisation, with both lay* and ordained* members, founded in 1928 in Madid by Saint* Josemaria Escriva de Balaguer to enable its members to seek holiness in everyday life and work.

Oratorians (Congregation of the Oratory) The Oratory* is a group of independent communities of priests*, living without taking vows, begun by Saint* Philip Neri (1515–95) in Rome in 1548, and officially recognised in 1583. Oratorians serve as priests* in parishes* and as chaplains*. Many are engaged in writing and teaching. Their churches* are frequently centres for high-quality liturgical* music and other cultural events.

Order (Latin *ordo* – a rank or dedicated group) A general term for communities of monks*, friars* or any kind of religious*.

Postulant (Latin *postulare* – to seek or ask) Someone undergoing a trial period in a community to discern whether he or she is to proceed to the novitiate*.

Prior (Latin *prior* – first) The superior* of a religious* house. In Benedictine* monasteries*, the assistant to the abbot*, or the superior of a smaller monastery* or priory*.

Priory In Benedictine* monasteries*, a monastery smaller than an abbey*, and governed by a prior*. All Carthusian* houses rank as priories.

Profession (Latin *professio* – to state one's faith* The act by which a religious* becomes a recognised member of a community. Most religious have a system of first (simple) and final (life) profession.

Province A subdivision, usually national, of a religious* order*.

Provincial The religious* superior* of a province. Many religious orders* group their members into provinces*.

Refectory In a monastery*, the dining hall of the monks* or nuns*, regarded as one of the most important places in the monastery. In Benedictine* monasteries, meals are eaten in silence, and during them the Rule of Saint Benedict* is read, together with Scripture* and other books.

Religious The general term for any member of a religious order*.

Rule (Latin *regula*) The written and oral customs, rules and general spirituality by which religious* live.

Rule of Saint Benedict The Rule*, the spirituality, set of rules, customs and regulations by which Benedictine* and many other communities of monks* and nuns* are generally inspired and governed. Saint* Benedict (*c*.480–550CE) became a hermit* in his youth and later on gathered disciples*, making monastic foundations in central Italy. Benedict probably wrote the Rule for his monastery* at Monte Cassino. The Rule of Saint Benedict is thought to be an abridgement of 'The Rule of the Master', an earlier Italian monastic rule of great severity, and shows great wisdom in its balance of authority and responsibility, moderation and encouragement. Within two hundred years of its composition it was adopted in many of the monasteries of northern Europe and has retained its pre-eminence, both for religious* and many lay* people, to this day.

Scapular (Latin *scapulae* – shoulder blades) Part of a monk's* or nun's* habit*, worn around the shoulders and hanging down back and front. The term also denotes a number of objects worn around the neck for religious purposes.

Sisters The term commonly used for members of female religious* orders*, though usually only applied to those not in enclosed* monasteries*. It describes many hundreds of different communities, usually engaged in pastoral*, educational, missionary* or social work. In the Middle Ages, women religious tended to be enclosed* and it was only in the sixteenth and seventeenth centuries that women adopted a more outgoing role in the Church*. Some communities date from this period, others were formed in the nineteenth century in order to provide for the educational and social needs of the European Church in the period following the French Revolution and the forced abolition of many of the Church's traditional charitable institutions. Similar groups were founded in the Americas to provide for the Church in the expanding territories of the United States and Canada.

Spiritual Exercises A term sometimes used to denote a retreat*, but it is properly applied to the procedure based on the book written by Saint* Ignatius Loyola which lays down a thirty-day process of Scripture* meditation*, prayer* and dialogue between the retreatant* and the spiritual director to provide a way of discernment and prayer* for the Society of Jesus* which he founded.

Superior A generic term to describe anyone who holds the position of leadership in a religious* community.

Veil (Latin *velum*) The traditional headgear of Benedictine* and other nuns*. It was modelled on the marriage* veil used in the late Roman period.

Virgin A class of female religious* who are dedicated by the bishop* to a life of solitude and prayer*.

Visitor The senior religious*, always from another community, who regularly visits and inspects the affairs of individual houses or monasteries*, to ensure discipline and observance of the rule*.

LITURGICAL BOOKS

The words of the prayers* and readings used at Mass* and the other liturgical* services* of the Church* are found in a series of liturgical books, officially recognised by the Church through the bishops* and the Holy See*. In this section the English title of the book is given first. The Latin title is given in brackets, together with a literal translation where the common English title differs.

The English translations used in the liturgy* are common, with some small variants, to the whole English-speaking world, and are prepared by the International Commission on English in the Liturgy (I.C.E.L.).

The Latin titles of some commonly used chant* books for services in Latin are found in the section on 'Music in the Liturgy', page 95.

Book of Blessings (*Liber Benedictionum*) A compendium of rites* for the blessing* of people, objects and places.

Breviary (Latin *brevis* – short, abbreviated) The title formerly given to the books containing the Liturgy of the Hours*. It is still a common way of referring to the Office*.

Divine Office (Latin *officium* – duty) The name often given to the Liturgy of the Hours*, the round of daily services* celebrated especially by priests* and religious*. The title was given to the English bishops'* translation of the Liturgy of the Hours* in 1974.

Lectionary (*Ordo Lectionum Missae* – Order of Readings for Mass) The order of the Scripture* readings for Sunday* and daily Mass* throughout the Year. For Sunday Mass, the lectionary works on the principle of reading through the whole of one of the Synoptic Gospels* throughout each year of a three-year cycle, Matthew* in the first year, Mark* in the second and Luke* in the third. The Gospel of John* is read in its entirety each year. At weekday masses also, whole books of Scripture are read through in the same way. For Sunday Mass, the lectionary usually provides an Old Testament* reading, responsorial psalm* and a New Testament* reading, usually a continuous reading from one of Saint Paul's* Letters*. In Ordinary Time* the Old Testament reading and the Gospel* have the same theme. At other times, all the readings are related. For weekdays, a single reading is read, with a responsorial psalm, before the Gospel. Some scriptural books are allotted to certain seasons*. In Eastertime* the Acts of the Apostles* is read in place of the Old Testament. The lectionary was put together as part of the reform of the liturgy* and the greater availability of Scripture in the worship* of the Church* which had been called for by the Second Vatican Council*.

Liturgy of the Hours (*Liturgia Horarum*) The proper title for the daily prayer* services* of the Church* as reformed after the Second Vatican Council* and the books that contain them. See also **Divine Office**

Missal (*Missale Romanum* – The Roman Missal) The collective title for the books used at Mass*: the lectionary* and the Missal or Sacramentary*.

Order for the Baptism of Infants* (*Ordo Baptismi Parvulorum*) See the section on 'Sacraments and Other Services', page 55.

Order of Christian Funerals* (*Ordo Exsequiarum* – Order of Funerals) See the section on 'Sacraments and Other Services', page 61.

Order of the Dedication of a Church and Altar (*Ordo Dedicationis Ecclesiae et Altaris*) Part of the Pontifical*. See **Dedication of a Church**

Psalter The book of psalms*, usually with the Old* and New Testament* canticles* included. The translation of the Book of Psalms* approved for use in the lectionary* and in the Divine Office* in the United Kingdom, Ireland and elsewhere is that prepared under the sponsorship of the Grail.

Rite of Anointing and Pastoral Care of the Sick* (*Ordo Unctionis Infirmorum eorumque Pastoralis Curae*) Contains all the rites* used with the sick and dying.

Rite for the Christian Initiation of Adults* (*Ritus Initiationis Christianae Adultorum*) The book describing the process and containing all the rites* for the preparation, baptism* and confirmation* of adults.

Rite of Confirmation* (*Ordo Confirmationis*) See the section on 'Sacraments and Other Services', page 55.

Rite of Marriage* (*Ordo Celebrandi Matrimonium*) See the sections on 'Sacraments and other services' and 'Canon Law on Marriage', pages 55 and 150.

Rite of Ordination* (*De Ordinatione Episcopi, Presbyterorum et Diaconorum* – concerning the ordination of the bishop*, presbyters* and deacons*) See the sections on 'Sacraments and Other Services' and 'Ministry', pages 55 and 113.

Rite of Penance* (*Ordo Paenitentiae*) The rites* used in the Sacrament of Penance* for both individual and communal liturgies*.

Roman pontifical (*Pontificale Romanum*) (Latin *pontifex* – 'bridge-builder' – a title from pagan* Rome, referring to the chief priest* of the state religion*) The collective term for the books that contain the rites* proper to bishops*, such as ordinations* and the dedication* of churches*.

Roman ritual (*Rituale Romanum*) The title for the group of books containing the prayers* used at the celebration* of the sacraments* of baptism*, marriage* and anointing*.

SIGNS AND EMBLEMS

There are many signs and emblems found as part of the ornamentation of churches*, on vessels used for worship*, vestments* and hangings, or as part of the architectural decoration. This section gives some of those most frequently employed.

Alpha/omega The first and last letters of the Greek alphabet, used by the Church* to name Christ* (Revelation* 1:8, 21:6) as the eternal* Lord*. The usage may come from Hebrew, where the first and last letters of the alphabet are the first and last letters of the word for 'truth'.

A.M.D.G. (Latin *ad maiorem Dei gloriam* – to the greater glory of God*) Often found in buildings as part of a dedication* inscription, or on articles used in worship*. The phrase is traditionally associated with Saint* Ignatius of Loyola and the Jesuits*.

Angel The emblem of Saint Matthew* the Apostle* and Evangelist*. See **Emblems of the evangelists**

Bull The emblem of Saint Luke* the Evangelist*. See **Emblems of the Evangelists**

Chalice and host See **Corpus Christi**

Chi-Rho The first two letters of the Greek word 'Christ*', written as X (Ch) and P (R), usually superimposed on each other.

Column One of the instruments of the Passion* of Christ* was the column* to which he was tied for scourging (Matthew* 27:26).

Corpus Christi The chalice* with the host* forms the emblem of the Eucharist* and especially of the Eucharistic* festival (Corpus Christi), instituted in the thirteenth century, of the body (and blood) of Christ*.

Cross The principal Christian* sign, the instrument of Christ's* crucifixion*. The Roman cross was an upright stake, to which was fixed a crossbeam, giving the shape of a 'T' to the cross. The condemned person carried this beam to the place of crucifixion, before being tied or nailed to it. Crosses come in many forms, of which the Greek* and Latin* are the most common.

Cross keys The emblem of Saint Peter*, to whom Christ* entrusted 'The keys of the kingdom of heaven* (Matthew* 16:19). The cross keys are an emblem of the papacy and are also found on coats of arms of bishops* (as successors of the apostles*) and dioceses* as well as churches* dedicated to Saint Peter.

Crown An emblem for Christ*, the 'King of kings'. The crown is also associated with martyrs* (Revelation* 4:4).

Crown of thorns One of the instruments of the Passion*, placed upon the head of Jesus* by the Roman soldiers (Matthew* 27:29).

D.O.M. (Latin *Deo Optimo Maximo* – to God* the best and greatest) A dedication found on memorials and buildings. Originally a pagan* Roman dedication to the god Jupiter and found on the Temple of Jupiter on the Capitol in Rome, it passed eventually into Christian* use.

Dove The emblem of the Holy Spirit*, who descended on Jesus* at his baptism* in the form of a dove (Matthew* 3:16).

Eagle The emblem of Saint John* the Apostle* and Evangelist*. See **Emblems of the evangelists**

Emblems of the evangelists The evangelists* Matthew*, Mark*, Luke* and John* were each given an emblem in Christian* art. These symbols* were based on animals found in the Book of Revelation* (Revelation 4:6–8). The symbol of Saint* Matthew is an angel*, Saint Mark is symbolised by a winged lion*, Saint Luke by a winged bull* and Saint John by a flying eagle*.

Fish (Greek *ichthus* – fish) An emblem of Christ*. The fish sign may derive from the Greek initial letters forming the acrostic 'Jesus* Christ, Son of God*, Saviour*'. The fish is used also to denote the Eucharist*, as fish feature in those miraculous feeding miracles which are thought to be eucharistic* texts (Matthew* 14:15–21).

131

Gridiron The emblem of Saint* Lawrence, deacon* and third-century Roman martyr*, killed by being roasted to death* on a fire.

Halo A golden disc or circle of light* placed in art above or around the head of Christ* or a saint*. In early Christian* art the halo was used to identify living people as well as saints. In the case of people still living, the halo was rectangular. In the making of icons*, the halo forms the circumference whose centre is the bridge of the nose of the face. See **Nimbus**

Heart (pierced) Originally a late medieval emblem of the Passion of Christ*, the pierced heart later became associated with the devotion* to the Sacred Heart* of Jesus*, popularised in the seventeenth century. The heart of Jesus, and the heart of Mary* (see Luke* 2:35), are both portrayed as pierced.

I.H.S. In Greek, these letters form the name of Jesus*. The letters are also interpreted to mean the words *Iesus Hominum Salvator* – Jesus, Saviour* of mankind, or the words *In Hoc Signo (vinces)* – 'In this sign (you will be victorious)', supposedly spoken in a dream to the Emperor Constantine the night before the decisive battle which gained him the emperorship. The 'sign' was the sign of the cross*.

I.N.R.I. The initial letters in Latin of the title *Iesus Nazarenus Rex Iudaeorum* – 'Jesus of Nazareth the King of the Jews', written in Hebrew, Greek and Latin on the cross* of Christ's* crucifixion* (John* 19:17–22).

Instruments of the Passion A collection of images* drawn from the New Testament* accounts of the Passion* of Jesus*. In medieval churches* there were often relics* of these instruments, and so they featured as images in the decoration of churches.

Lamb The emblem of Saint John the Baptist*, who proclaimed Jesus* as the Lamb* of God* (John* 1:29); also a symbol of some female virgins who were martyrs*, such as Saint* Agnes, the third-century Roman martyr.

Lilies White lilies in a pot are associated with virginity, and in particular with Our Lady*. They are often found in pictures of the Annunciation*.

Lion The winged lion is the emblem of Saint Mark*, the Evangelist*. See **Emblems of the evangelists**

M.R. The first letters of the Latin *Maria Regina* – 'Mary*, Queen', usually written superimposed. They are probably taken from the Antiphon* to Our Lady* *Salve Regina* – 'Hail, holy* Queen'.

Nails One of the instruments of the Passion*, the nails fastened Jesus* to the cross*. In Roman crucifixions*, the nails were probably driven through the wrists and the ankles of the victim.

Palm leaves An emblem associated with martyrs* (see Revelation* 7:9).

Paschal lamb The Gospel of John* interprets Jesus'* death* as a new Passover* sacrifice*, and portrays Jesus as the passover lamb* (John 19:36 and 1:35). The Book of Revelation* uses this image also (Revelation 5:6, 7:17, 14:1). In the Middle Ages, the lamb came to be associated also with Saint John the Baptist* (John 1:35).

Pelican The image of the pelican feeding her young with blood from her own breast is associated with the Eucharist*. The legend was that the pelican so loved her chicks that she would give her lifeblood to feed them. A medieval hymn* for Corpus Christi* speaks of Christ* as *pie pellicane* – 'loving pelican'.

Purse One of the instruments of the Passion*, the purse refers to the thirty pieces of silver received by Judas Iscariot* as a price for betraying Jesus* (Matthew* 26:14–16).

R.I.P. The initial letters of the Latin *Requiescat In Pace* – 'may he/she rest in peace'. This monogram is often seen on gravestones and tombs*. Catholics* also use it as a prayer* for the departed.

Rose An emblem of the Virgin Mary*, who was invoked under the title of 'Mystical Rose'.

Saltire A cross* made of two diagonally intersecting arms. It is the emblem of Saint Andrew*, who according to legend was crucified at Patras in Greece.

Scallop shell An emblem associated with pilgrimage*, especially to the shrine* of Saint*

James at Compostela, in northern Spain. The reputed body of Saint James was enshrined in the cathedral*. Compostela was one of the most popular medieval pilgrimages and is still visited by pilgrims*.

Seamless robe One of the instruments of the Passion* was the one-piece robe for which the soldiers cast lots (John* 19:23–4).

Ship An emblem of the Church*, possibly based on the ancient use of Noah's Ark as an image of the Church – the 'Ark of Salvation* – or else on the fishing boat used by the Apostle* Peter*.

Skull and crossbones The emblem of death* and resurrection*, often found on gravestones, also on the crucifix* where it is a reference to Golgotha, the 'Place of the Skull' (Matthew* 27:33). The cross* is seen to be rising from the skull, as the risen life of Jesus* arose from death.

Spear One of the instruments of the Passion* was the spear with which Jesus* was pierced to make sure he was already dead (John* 19:33, 34).

Sword An image* associated with Saint Paul*, possibly deriving from his image of the 'sword of the Spirit*' (Ephesians* 6:17), or from the sword with which, as a Roman citizen, he would have been beheaded.

Wheat ears and grapes An emblem of the Eucharist* denoting bread* and wine*.

Whip One of the instruments of the Passion* was the whip with which Jesus* was scourged (Matthew* 27:26).

OUR LADY AND THE SAINTS

The Saints (Latin *sanctus* – holy)

The Catholic* Church* honours the saints* – holy* and significant men and women from the New Testament* and from the history of the Church. Those considered as saints are people who have either given their life as martyrs*, or lived exemplary Christian* lives. Old Testament* saints such as Adam*, the patriarchs* and some of the prophets* are also honoured in the same way as saints.

In the early Church, martyrs were given great honour. Records of their 'passion*' (death*) were kept and their place of burial* was remembered and venerated. Each year the anniversary of their martyrdom* was celebrated. Each local Church had its own martyrs, though some, such as the Apostles* Peter* and Paul* in Rome, were venerated more widely.

After the fourth century, it became customary to build churches over martyrs' graves*, such as the Basilica* of Saint Peter in Rome, and Saint Paul-Outside-the-Walls, both built by the Emperor Constantine. Some of these were intended as gathering places for pilgrims* rather than as churches for regular celebration* of the Eucharist*.

By the sixth century, people other than martyrs began to be revered as 'saints'. These were often bishops*, monks* or founders of monasteries*. In the twelfth century, the popes* instituted the process of 'canonisation*' to declare formally that someone was a saint, and therefore might be named and celebrated in the liturgy*.

Saints are honoured in different ways in the liturgy. Some are of such significance that their feast* day is observed by the whole Church, others are celebrated in particular places only. Dioceses* and religious* orders* have their own local saints.

Catholics* often pray to saints to act as their 'sponsor*' or 'intercede' for them with God*. Many Catholics have a saint's name given to them at baptism*. Relics* of saints are honoured and their birthplace and place of death are sometimes places of pilgrimage*.

Some saints act as 'patrons' for different types of trade, profession or person. Many countries also have a patron saint* or 'protector'. Some saints are looked to for help in particular circumstances. Saint Anthony (a thirteenth-century Franciscan* saint) is appealed to by people who have lost things. Saint Jude is the saint of lost causes. Many saints have emblems to identify them (See the section on 'Signs and Emblems', page 130.

Our Lady

Mary*, the Virgin* Mother of Jesus*, is the most important of the saints*. She is celebrated in the liturgy* under a number of titles. The most significant theologically is that of 'Mother of God'* but she is also known as 'the Blessed Virgin Mary'* or 'the Ever-Virgin Mary', or simply 'Our Lady'. Mary occupies a key role in the New Testament*. She consents to be the mother of Jesus (Luke* 2:26–38); she is greeted by Elizabeth her cousin as 'blessed* among women' (Luke 1:39–45); she speaks the Magnificat*, she bears Jesus and presents him in the Temple (Luke 2:22–35). She is present at the first of Jesus' signs* of his divine glory at Cana in Galilee (John* 2:1–12) where he changes water* into wine*. Mary is present at the foot of the cross* and Jesus entrusts her to the disciple* John* as his mother (John 19:25–7). She is present with the apostles* in the upper room for Pentecost* (Acts* 1:14).

In early Christian* legend, Mary was the daughter of Joachim*, a Temple priest*, and Anna*. Anna conceived her when well past the age of childbearing. In legend too, after Jesus on the cross had given her into the care of John (John 19:27) Mary lived with him at Ephesus. The moment of her death* was witnessed by the apostles, who had been miraculously gathered together for the event.

In Church teaching, Mary conceived and gave birth to Christ while still a virgin and remained so after his birth. Also, she is regarded as the first of those whom Christ* has redeemed by his death and resurrection*. This applies to her both at the beginning and end of her life. At her conception in her mother's womb she was saved from original sin* (see **Immaculate Conception**), while at her death she was assumed into heaven*, body and soul* (see **Assumption of the Blessed Virgin Mary**).

There are several feasts* of Mary during the year. The most important are: the Mother of God* (1 January), the Assumption* (15 August), and the Immaculate Conception* (8 December).

Two months of the year are dedicated specially to Mary, May ('Mary's month') and October (the month of the Rosary*).

There are several major shrines* of Our Lady, where pilgrims* gather in large numbers. Details of four of the most important are given in the word list below.

Word List

Adam (Hebrew for 'man made of the earth') The ancestor of humankind. According to the second creation myth (Genesis* 2:7), God* formed man out of clay. Adam fell through his disobedience in eating the fruit of the tree God had prohibited him from eating. Early Christian* tradition* portrayed him as being redeemed, together with Eve*, by the Risen Christ's* descent among the dead. Saint Paul* names Christ as the 'Second Adam' (Romans* 5:12–21), thus reversing a Jewish tradition that the first Adam had a 'prototype' created in heaven*.

All Saints The feast* of All Saints (1 November) is celebrated to honour every saint*, whether known or unknown. Originally a feast of martyrs*, the feast is now kept as a celebration* of all the 'citizens of the heavenly Jerusalem' (Revelation* chapters 21 and 22).

Andrew, Saint, Apostle The brother of Saint Peter* and among those first called by Jesus*. He is said to have suffered martyrdom* in Greece and is a patron saint of Scotland and Russia.

Anna Early Christian* legend gives Anna as the name of the mother of the Blessed Virgin Mary*.

Apostle (Greek *apostolos* – someone sent) The name given to each of twelve men chosen by Jesus* from his disciples* to be most closely associated with his ministry*. The names of the Twelve are: Peter* (originally called Simon) and Andrew* his brother; James the son of Zebedee and his brother John*; Philip, Bartholomew, Thomas, Matthew* (originally called Levi); James son of Alphaeus, Thaddeus (also known as Jude), Simon the Zealot and Judas Iscariot.

Assumption (Late Latin *assumere* – to take up) According to tradition*, the Blessed Virgin Mary* was taken up into heaven* at her death*, because of her special place as the Mother of God*. The legend speaks of the twelve apostles* being summoned by angels* to Ephesus to witness her death, and finding the coffin empty. The Assumption was proclaimed a dogma* of the Catholic* Church* by Pope* Pius XII in 1950.

Beatification (Latin *beatus* – blessed) A stage in the process of canonisation* where the candidate is declared 'blessed*' and able to be celebrated in the liturgy*.

Blessed A title given to some saints*; also the title given to one who is awaiting canonisation*.

Blessed Virgin Mary A title of Mary*, used in liturgical* prayer* (often coupled with the title 'Mother of God'*), and emphasising her virginal conception and childbearing of Jesus*.

Canonisation (Greek *kanon* – rule) The process by which someone is declared a saint*. It has three stages. If there is a demand, or if someone is already being venerated as a holy* person, they may be considered a candidate for canonisation. The life and writings of the candidate are examined. If the examination is favourable, the candidate may be declared 'venerable*', and after a further examination, 'blessed*'. Only then, after further scrutiny, can he or she be declared a saint. In addition to the examination of the candidate, something must be proved to indicate that he or she is truly 'with God*' and an intercessor for us. This is usually a medical cure or other intervention that cannot be explained by conventional scientific knowledge. The Pope* will finally canonise the individual and declare that the candidate is a saint.

Confessor (Latin *confiteri* – to profess the faith) Someone who has given especial witness to Christ* without being a martyr*.

Czestochowa, Marian Shrine In Poland, the Monastery* of Jasna Gora which houses the Miraculous Ikon* of Our Lady*, the Black Madonna, and is one of the great European places of pilgrimage*.

Disciple (Latin *discipulus* – one who listens and learns) The term used in the Gospels* of the close companions of Jesus*. Some of these he chose as apostles*.

Evangelist (Greek *evangelion* – gospel, good news) Saints Matthew*, Mark*, Luke* and John* whose names are linked to the four Gospels*. Tradition* has it that Matthew recorded his Gospel in a Jewish milieu; that Mark was the disciple* of Peter*; Luke is identified with the author of Acts* and was the travelling companion of Saint Paul*; John is identified with the 'Beloved Disciple' of the Fourth Gospel (John 19:26).

THE SANCTIFYING CHURCH

Fatima A shrine* of Our Lady* near Lisbon in Portugal, the site of her appearance in 1917 to three children. The Church* affirmed the authenticity of the apparitions in 1930. The 'message' of Fatima encourages recitation of the rosary*, works of asceticism* and the consecration* of Russia to the Sacred Heart*.

Feast (Latin *festum* – a festival) The day dedicated to the celebration* of some aspect of the Christian* faith*, or to a saint*.

Guadaloupe A Mexican shrine* of Our Lady*. In 1531, the Blessed Virgin Mary* appeared to Juan Diego, on Tepeyac Hill near Mexico City. A life-size image* of Our Lady, painted to resemble a Mexican woman, was miraculously imprinted on his cloak*. This painting is now housed in the shrine. The Church* in the Americas now celebrates a feast* in honour of Our Lady of Guadaloupe as 'Mother of the Americas' on 12 December.

Immaculate Conception A feast* of the conception of the Blessed Virgin Mary* in the womb of Saint Anne*, her mother, was celebrated on 8 December from some time in the Middle Ages. The doctrine* that she was 'immaculately conceived', i.e., conceived without Original Sin*, emerged in the medieval period (though not everyone agreed with it) and was proclaimed as binding on the whole Church* by Pope* Pius IX in 1854.

Intercession (Latin *intercedere* – to be an advocate) The Risen Christ* is our primary 'intercessor' with the Father*. Early in the history of the Church*, however, people began to venerate the saints* as people who might speak up or intercede for them with Christ.

Joachim According to tradition* going back to the second century CE, Joachim was a Temple priest* and the father of the Blessed Virgin Mary*. The story of Mary's* birth is possibly modelled on that of John the Baptist* in Luke* 1.

John The 'disciple* Jesus* loved' (John* 19:26). John is named as the author of the Fourth Gospel. According to some early Christian* traditions*, he lived and died at Ephesus.

John the Baptist A kinsman of Jesus*, John 'the Baptiser' exercised a preaching and baptising ministry* by the River Jordan at the beginning of the public ministry of Jesus. Jesus was baptised by him (Matthew* 3:13–17) and at his baptism* he was revealed as God's* Son* by the Holy Spirit* who rested upon him. John was beheaded by Herod at the request of his wife (Matthew 14:3–12). In the Roman liturgy*, John has two feast* days, his birth on 24 June and his martyrdom* on 29 August.

La Salette A French shrine* of the Blessed Virgin Mary*, the site of her reputed apparitions in 1846, recognised as authentic by the Church* in 1851. The chief message of the apparitions was a call to penance* on the part of Christians*.

Lourdes A French shrine* of the Blessed Virgin Mary*. In 1858, the Blessed Virgin Mary appeared some eighteen times to a young woman, Bernadette Soubirous, announcing herself as 'the Immaculate Conception*'. The Church* approved the cult in 1862. The shrine at Lourdes is frequented by many pilgrims*, many of whom come to seek healing* in the waters* of the Lourdes Grotto where the apparitions took place.

Mark, Saint, Evangelist The second of the four Gospels is attributed to Mark, whom early tradition names as the companion of Peter. See Mark, page 108

Martyr (Greek *martus* – witness) One who accepts death* rather than deny faith* in Christ*. The idea of martyrdom* goes back to the Jewish Maccabees*, but

Christianity has developed its own cult of martyrs, often centred on their tombs* or relics*.

Martyrdom (Greek *martus* – witness) The act of laying down one's life for the Christian* faith*.

Martyrology (Greek *martus* – witness, and *logos* – account) A calendar list of all the saints* celebrated on each day during the course of a year, together with an account of their life and death*.

Matthew, Saint, Apostle and Evangelist Matthew is mentioned in the Gospel of Matthew* (9:9) as a tax collector, called to be a disciple.

Michael, the Archangel One of the archangels*, commemorated by name on 29 September.

Mother of God The principal theological title of Mary*, awarded her at the Council* of Ephesus, reflecting her vocation* as Mother of Christ*, in whom divine and human natures were united in one single person.

Our Lady A popular title of the Blessed Virgin Mary* which emerged in Europe in the Middle Ages.

Passion (Latin *passio* – suffering) Usually applied to the sufferings of Christ*; the documents recording the deaths* of some martyrs* are also referred to as 'passions'.

Patriarch (Greek *pater* – father, and *archos* – original) The title given to Abraham, Isaac and Jacob, the ancestors of the Jewish, Christian* and Moslem faiths.

Patron saint The saint* after whom a church* is named, or the saint having a connection with a particular nation or group.

Paul See **Saint Paul**

Peter See **Saint Peter**

Pilgrimage A journey to a holy* place undertaken as a religious act. The earliest pilgrimages, in the late third and the fourth centuries CE, were to Jerusalem, where in the fourth century the Emperor Constantine built a basilica* on the site of the crucifixion* and resurrection* of Christ*. With the Islamic conquest of Palestine in the seventh century, pilgrims* found it harder to visit Jerusalem, and sites elsewhere became popular. Many pilgrimage places appeared in Europe, such as that of Saint* James at Compostela* in Spain (eleventh century). In the Middle Ages, each country had many places of pilgrimage, increasingly associated with the Blessed Virgin Mary*. Many thousands of Christians* still make pilgrimages to the Holy Land and to the shrines* of Our Lady*.

Saint Paul, Apostle of the Gentiles Originally named Saul, a Jewish scholar of Tarsus in Asia Minor, Paul was on his way to Damascus to persecute Christians* when he saw a vision of the risen Christ* and was converted to the new faith*. He journeyed throughout the Mediterranean, founding Christian* churches*, to whom he later addressed his Letters*. These reveal him to be the first great Christian theologian*. By tradition* he was executed at Rome in about 65CE. According to tradition, his remains rest within the Basilica* of Saint-Paul-Outside-the-Walls in Rome.

Saint Peter, first of the apostles Simon, chosen by Jesus* as the first among the apostles*, and named 'Peter' (the Rock) because of his naming of Jesus as the Messiah* (Matthew* 16:18). He is associated with two Letters* contained in the New Testament*. By tradition* he went to Rome where he was martyred* in about 65CE. Tradition locates his remains as enshrined on the Vatican* Hill, within the present Saint Peter's Basilica*.

THE SANCTIFYING CHURCH

Shrines of Our Lady in Great Britain Many places in Britain are associated from pre-Reformation* times with pilgrimages* to the Blessed Virgin Mary*. Three of the most important are: Walsingham in Norfolk (where the reputed House of Mary* was venerated from the eleventh century), Haddington near Edinburgh and Cardigan (Our Lady* of the Taper) in Wales.

Thomas Aquinas, Saint (*c.*1225–74) The great teacher and theologian* of the thirteenth-century Dominican* community. He studied and taught at Paris, Orvieto and Rome and left two important works on theology: the *Suma Theologiae* and the *Suma Contra Gentiles*. Canonised* in 1323 and declared a doctor of the Church in 1567. His way of doing theology has influenced the teaching and study of it ever since his death.

Virgin A category of saint*.

Widow A category of saint*.

PART FOUR

THE GOVERNING CHURCH

ORGANISATION AND
GOVERNANCE

The Catholic* Church* is led and served by an ordained* ministry*, received from the apostles* and the first Christian* communities. This consists of bishops*, priests* and deacons*. The duty of teaching in the name of Christ*, presiding at the celebration* of the sacraments* and the pastoral* leadership of the Church is entrusted to them. The Second Vatican Council* gives first place to the college of bishops* in union with the Pope* as successor of Saint Peter*. The basic expression of the universal Church is the 'local church'* – the diocese* – with its priests, deacons and lay* people gathered round the bishop. (See the section on 'Ministry', page 113.)

That ordained ministry governs the Church under what is known as Canon Law*. This chapter deals with the canonical or legal side of Church government. The diocesan bishop* may have 'coadjutor* or auxiliary bishops*. He will have senior priests as vicar general,* episcopal vicar* and judicial vicar*. He will have a council of priests*, a college of consultors* and, in some dioceses, a chapter* of canons*.

The diocesan bishop is assisted by priests, who preside over the local gatherings of Catholics* in the diocese. These are known as parishes*. Within the parish, there may be a permanent deacon*. There will be other, non-ordained, ministers*. Canon Law obliges each parish to have a finance committee. There may be a parish pastoral council*.

Dioceses, the basic expression of the Church, are grouped in and served by national or regional groupings of bishops, known as the episcopal conference*. The conference itself will have agencies acting for the good of the Church in its territory.

Bishops work as a 'college*' in communion* with the Pope*, who presides over the whole Church. Like his fellow bishops, the Pope is bishop of a diocese, that of Rome.

The Pope is assisted by cardinals*. The 'college of cardinals*' mostly consists of bishops of major dioceses throughout the world, together with the heads of the Vatican* departments or 'congregations*' that undertake the day-to-day management of the universal Church (see **Roman Curia**). The cardinals traditionally elect the Pope.

Apostolic delegate The diplomatic representative of the apostolic see* to a particular nation.

THE GOVERNING CHURCH

Apostolic nuncio (Latin *nuntiare* – to announce) The highest rank of diplomatic representation of the apostolic see*. See **Nuncio**

Apostolic penitentiary A tribunal* of the Holy See*, concerned with matters relating to the Sacrament of Penance* and Indulgences*.

Apostolic see The name given to the dioceses* that claimed an apostle* as their first bishop*. Nowadays among Catholics* the term is used only to describe the See* of Rome*. See **Holy See**

Apostolic Signatura A tribunal* of the Holy See*, the Church's* highest court, also in charge of the procedure for the canonisation* of saints*.

Arch- (Greek *archi-* – chief) The prefix denoting that the person so described is first in a group, e.g., archbishop*.

Archbishop The bishop* who has oversight of a group of dioceses* known as a province*. Archbishops are robed as bishops, entitled 'The Most Reverend*' and addressed as 'Your Excellency', sometimes 'Your Grace'.

Archdiocese (Greek *archi-* – chief, and see **Diocese**) The diocese* which has an archbishop*.

Archpriest (Greek *archi-* – chief) A term used for the senior priest* (or dean) at a cathedral*. The term is sometimes used for the dean* or vicar forane* in a deanery*.

Area bishop A bishop* within a diocese who has a particular area of that diocese assigned to him.

Assistant priest A priest* who serves a parish*, but not as parish priest* (see also **Curate**). In the United States, the term is 'parochial* vicar' or 'associate pastor*'.

Auditor (Latin *audire* – to hear) One who takes down evidence in a case conducted under Canon Law*.

Auxiliary bishop A bishop* who assists the diocesan bishop* when the diocese* is large or for some other reason. An auxiliary usually has the title of an ancient (but no longer functioning) diocese assigned to him. Auxiliary bishops have the same title as diocesan bishops, 'The Right Reverend*' (in Ireland and some other places 'The Most Reverend'), and are addressed as 'Your Excellency' or 'My Lord'.

Bishopric ('-ric' cf. German *reich* – realm) The place, status and duty of being a bishop*.

Cathedral administrator The title given to the parish priest* of a Catholic* cathedral* in the United Kingdom. The administrator may also be known as the dean.

Canon (Greek *kanon* – rule*) In the Middle Ages and after, a priest* who lived at the cathedral* of the diocese* and shared the responsibility for its liturgy* and upkeep. Now the title is used for senior priests in a diocese who do not necessarily live at the cathedral. Canons have special dress (see page 117), use the same title as priests, 'The Reverend*', and may be addressed as 'Canon'. Many dioceses, e.g., in the USA, do not have canons.

Canon (Greek *kanon* – rule*) A law of the Church. See **Canon Law**.

Canonical (Greek *kanon* – rule) Of or pertaining to Canon Law*.

Canon Law (Greek *kanon* – rule*) A term denoting the law of the Church*. Saint Paul's* Letters* contain some of the earliest pieces of Church law. Over the centuries, collections of laws (often called 'decretals') were made. The first comprehensive 'Code' was issued (promulgated) in 1917. It contained 2414 'canons'* or laws. The present Code was issued in 1983 and contains 1752 canons.

Canon Law applies to everyone in the Church, whether ordained*, religious* or lay* people. It regulates most aspects of the Church's life and work. The Code (entitled in English translation *The Code of Canon Law*) is divided into three sections, concerning the teaching, sanctifying and governing roles of the Church. There is Canon Law on how the Church is governed, how the sacraments* are celebrated, responsibilities of bishops*, priests* and deacons*, what its ministers* do and how they live, how Church property and assets are to be managed and how legal hearings are to be conducted.

The 1983 Code is divided into seven sections: General Norms, The People of God*, The Teaching Office of the Church, The Sanctifying Office of the Church, The Temporal Goods of the Church, Sanctions in the Church, Processes (trials, hearings etc.).

Canon penitentiary A member of the chapter* of canons* responsible for certain aspects of the Sacrament of Penance*.

Cardinal (Latin *cardo* – hinge, linchpin) Originally, the cardinals were the priests* and deacons* of the principal churches* of the city of Rome* and some local bishops*. Nowadays a cardinal is always a bishop, usually one who either leads a major diocese* somewhere in the world, or works in Rome as a member of the Roman Curia*. Cardinals are the principal collaborators of the Pope*, and his electors. Cardinals robe in red and are titled and addressed as 'His/Your Eminence'.

Celibacy (Latin *caelibatus* – heavenly state) The unmarried, chaste state required (as a rule) since the twelfth century for priests* and bishops*. Originally only monks* and nuns* were celibate, but celibacy was recommended for clergy* generally from about the fourth century. Where priests and deacons* are married and become widowed, they may not remarry and remain in the ministry*.

Censure In Canon Law*, the penalty for a grave offence. Excommunication, interdict* and suspension* are all censures.

Chancellor The official appointed to draw up and keep the archives of the diocesan curia*.

Chaplain (Late Latin *capellanus* – priest* assigned to a chapel*) A priest appointed to a particular, non-parochial, pastoral* post, e.g.: to a bishop*, a college, the armed forces, a hospital, a workplace, a prison, a school, or university. Chaplains, if priests, are styled 'The Reverend*' and addressed as 'Father*'. Sometimes, lay* people are appointed as 'lay chaplains'.

Chapter of canons (Latin *capitulum* – a portion of Scripture*, and Greek *kanon* – rule*). The title given to canons* as a body. Originally their meetings began with a reading from Scripture.

Clergy (root in Greek *klerous* – drawing by lots) Bishops*, priests* and deacons* ordained* to ministry* in the Church*.

Clerical state (Latin *clericus* – one in orders*) The canonical state of those in the ordained* ministry*. Formal admission to the clerical state is made at ordination* to the diaconate*.

Coadjutor bishop The bishop* who assists the diocesan* bishop in the case of illness or incapacity. A coadjutor has the right to succeed the bishop whom he assists. Title: 'The Right Reverend*' (in Ireland and some other places 'The Most Reverend'). Address: 'Your Excellency' or 'My Lord'.

Code (Latin *codex* – book) The title given to the collection of Church law or Canon Law*.

College of bishops The name given to the worldwide community of bishops* in communion* with the Pope*.

College of consultors A group of priests* chosen by the bishop*, which he is obliged to convene as an advisory committee in the diocese*.

Congregation (Latin prefix *con* – together, and *grex* – flock) The term used to describe the gathering of those who worship* in church*. In the Catholic* Church* 'congregation' is also the name given to many bodies of religious* men and women, and also to the departments of the Roman Curia*.

Competent In Canon Law*, the person or body charged by the Church* with the administration of any particular matter.

Council of priests Also known as the senate of priests* or presbyteral council; a body which a bishop* must convene according to Canon Law* as a means for consulting the clergy* of his diocese*.

Curate (medieval Latin *cura animarum* – care of souls*) The priest* who assists the parish priest* in the 'cure'* or care of the parish*. See **Assistant priest**

Cure (Latin *cura* – care) A spiritual duty, i.e., in caring for members of a parish* the parish priest* has the 'cure of souls*'.

Curia (Latin for 'court') The administration of a diocese*, or of the whole Church* (see **Roman Curia**).

Deacon See the section on 'Ministry', page 113.

Dean (Latin *decem* – ten) The priest* who has oversight of a group of parish* clergy* (see **Vicar forane**). The term is sometimes used of priests having charge of cathedral* churches and parishes.

Deanery The term for the group of priests* and parishes* under the oversight of the dean*.

Deanery pastoral council The consultative body which may be set up in a deanery*, consisting of both ordained* and non-ordained members.

Decree (Latin *decretum* – an order) The means whereby a bishop* or ordinary* formally expresses their intention and orders a particular course of action.

Diocesan bishop The bishop of a diocese, as opposed to a suffragan bishop*.

Diocesan pastoral council A body called by the bishop* and comprising clergy* and lay* people to discuss and make recommendations for pastoral* action in the diocese*.

Diocesan synod A council* composed of ex-officio and other clergy* with chosen lay* people, called by the bishop* where appropriate.

Diocese (Greek *dioikesis* – a territory under government) The group of parishes* or territory under the leadership of a bishop*. The name was, in Roman times, used to denote a territory of the Empire.

Episcopal conference (bishops' conference) The meeting of all the bishops* of a given region or nation.

Episcopal council The meeting of the bishop* and vicar(s) general*.

Episcopal vicar The title given to the priest* appointed by the bishop* with special responsibility in the diocese*, e.g., a 'vicar for religious*' with oversight of all religious communities of the diocese.

Episcopate The status and duty of a bishop*, also used to refer to the period of office of a bishop.

Faculty (Latin *facultas* – opportunity) Written permission granted by the ordinary* for something to take place, e.g., 'faculties' granted to ordained* and non-ordained ministers* to exercise their ministry*.

Father The proper address and title for priests* monks* and religious*, now usually employed as the term of address for all priests.

First instance A canonical court whose judgement is subject to scrutiny by a higher court.

Honorary canon A priest* given the rank of canon though not a member of the chapter of canons* of the diocese*.

Impeded The state of a diocese* if the bishop* is completely unable (even by letter) to exercise his ministry* through imprisonment, exile or incapacity.

Installation (Latin *stallium* – seat) The word used to describe the act by which someone, e.g., a bishop* or parish priest*, enters formally into a particular ministry*.

Interdict (Latin *interdico* – to forbid) In Canon Law* a penalty that presents participation in the liturgy* or reception of the sacraments*.

Interregnum (Latin *inter regnum* – between reign) A term in common usage describing the interval between the resignation or death* of an office holder and the installation* of a successor.

Judicial vicar The official of the diocesan curia* who looks after the canonical/ legal affairs of the diocese*.

Local church The term used after the Second Vatican Council* to describe the diocese*, the Church* gathered round the bishop*, also known as the 'particular church*'.

Local ordinary See **Ordinary**

Metropolitan (Greek *meter* – mother, and *polis* – city) A title for an archbishop*, or for his see*.

Metropolitan tribunal Under Canon Law*, the court set up in an archdiocese* to assess cases tried by diocesan courts.

Minister See the section on 'Ministry', page 113.

Moderator (Latin *moderare* – to govern) The official who heads the diocesan* curia* in some dioceses.

Nuncio (Latin *nuntiare* – to announce) The ambassader of the Holy See* to a state government. The position of nuncio is the highest form of papal representation.

Officialis (Latin for 'office holder') See **Judicial vicar**

Ordained See under the section on 'Ministry', page 113.

Order, religious See **Order**

Ordinand (Latin *ordinare* – to place in an order, to ordain*) A candidate for ordination*. See under the section on 'Ministry', page 113.

Ordinary (Latin *ordinarius* – the one who orders) A member of the clergy* exercising the jurisdiction which is an inseparable part of his ministry*. The bishop* is the ordinary in the diocese, i.e., the one to whom the duty of teaching, sanctifying (celebrating the sacraments*) and governing is ultimately entrusted.

Ordination See the section on 'Ministry', page 113.

Papacy (Latin *papa* – Pope) The institution of the Pope* and central governing authority in the Church*.

Parish (Greek *paroikia* – those dwelling close together) The name given to the Catholic* people in a given place under the care usually of a priest*, also used as a term denoting the territory of the parish.

Parish administrator A priest* appointed by the bishop* in case of vacancy in a parish* or incapacity of the parish priest*.

Parish church The principal church* building of a parish*.

Parish council A deliberative and advisory body representing the members of the parish* (sometimes known as 'parish pastoral council').

Parish priest The priest* appointed by the bishop* to serve a particular parish*. Often abbreviated as 'PP' and titled as priests, 'The Reverend*', addressed as 'Father*'. In the United States and elsewhere the term is 'Pastor*'.

Pope (Greek/Latin *papa* – father) The chief bishop* of the Catholic* Church*, the Bishop of Rome. The popes trace their descent back to Saint Peter*, the leader of the apostles*. The full title of the Pope is 'Bishop of Rome, Vicar* of Jesus* Christ*, Successor of Saint Peter*, Prince of the Apostles, Supreme Pastor* of the Universal Church, Patriarch* of the West, Primate* of Italy, Archbishop* and Metropolitan* of the Roman Province*, Sovereign of the State of the Vatican* City'. The Pope is titled and addressed as 'His/Your Holiness'.

Priest-in-charge The priest* appointed to administer a parish* in the absence of a formally named parish priest*.

Prelate (Latin *prae-latus* – placed in front) A title denoting senior clergy*, usually an honorary title and originally applied to those associated with the papal* court. See **Monsignor**

Presbyter See the section on 'Ministry', page 113.

Presbytery (Greek *presbyter* – elder) A title for the residence of the parish priest*.

Priest See the section on 'Ministry', page 113.

Primate (Latin *primus* – first) A term occasionally used of the chief archbishop* of a collection of provinces*.

Province A collection of dioceses* and bishops* under the general oversight of an archbishop*.

Promoter of the faith The official within the Holy See* who investigates any objections raised in a case for canonisation*; known popularly as the 'Devil's Advocate'.

Propaganda Fide (Propagation of the Faith) (Latin *propagare* – to diffuse, and *fides* – faith) The department of the Roman Curia* with responsibility for missions*, now known as the Sacred Congregation* for the Evangelisation* of Peoples.

Rector (Latin *rector* – one who governs) The priest* in charge of a church* that is not a parish* or a monastery* church. A place of pilgrimage*, for instance, may have a rector. The term is also used of the priest who is in overall charge of a seminary* or Catholic* university.

Rectory Especially in the United States, the place of residence of a parish priest*.

Registers The Council of Trent* obliged parishes* to keep registers of marriage*, baptism* and burial*. Registers are now kept of adult converts also, as part of the Rite for the Christian Initiation of Adults*.

Reverend (Latin *reverendus* – worthy of reverence) The usual title for ordained* ministers*.

Roman Curia (Latin *curia* – court) the central administration of the Church*. The Curia consists of the Secretariat of State (responsible for the general affairs of the Church and the overseas diplomatic representation of the Vatican*), nine 'congregations*': Doctrine* of the Faith* (teaching of the Church), Eastern Churches, Sacraments* and Divine Worship*, Causes of Saints* (canonisation* processes), Bishops*, Evangelisation* of Peoples (missions*), Clergy*, Institutes of Consecrated Life and Societies of Apostolic* Life (religious* communities) and Catholic* Education (universities, seminaries* and schools). In addition to the congregations there are three 'tribunals*: the Apostolic Penitentiary*, the Apostolic Segnatura* and the Roman Rota*. Also there are five 'offices' – the Apostolic Camera*, the Prefecture for the Economic Affairs of the Holy See, the Administration of the Patrimony of the Holy See (Vatican Heritage), the Prefecture of the Papal Household, the Statistical Office of the Church. There are also eleven Pontifical Councils: Laity, Christian Unity, the Family, Justice and Peace, 'Cor Unum' (the Papal Charity organization), Pastoral Care of Migrants and Itinerants, Pastoral Care of Health Workers, The Interpretation of Law, Inter-Religious Dialogue, Culture, Social Communication. Finally, there is an office for the Synod of Bishops* and a Vatican* Press Office.

Roman Rota A tribunal* of the Holy See*, forming a court of higher instance and appeal (see **First instance**). The Rota also conducts a school of jurisprudence.

Second Vatican Council See the section on 'Creeds and Councils', page 49.

See (Latin *sedes* – seat) The cathedra*, or seat, of the bishop*. The term is also used to denote a diocese*, or the town where the cathedral* is situated.

Simony The illegal act of purchasing ecclesiastical* office*. The term arises from the story of Simon the Magician (see Acts* 8:18–24).

Stipend (Latin *stips* – offering, and *pendere* – to pay) The income of the clergy*.

Stole fees The offering which may be given to the priest* at the celebration* of a sacrament* such as baptism*, when the stole* is worn.

Suffragan bishop (Latin *suffragari* – to support by vote) The term used to describe the bishops* of a province*. Suffragan bishops have the same title and address as bishops, 'The Right Reverend*' (In Ireland and elsewhere 'The Most Reverend'), and are addressed as 'Your Excellency' or 'My Lord'.

Suspension The formal prevention of a minister*, in the event of serious misdemeanour, from the exercise of his functions.

Synod (Greek *synodos* – a meeting) A deliberative gathering of the Church*. Bishops* meet in synod with the Pope* every few years; in each diocese* the bishop is advised by a synod of priests*.

Venerable (Latin *venerabilis* – worthy of reverence) The title given at the beginning of the process of canonisation* to one who is not yet a saint.

Vicar (Latin *vicarius* – substitute) A priest* appointed by the bishop* with special responsibilities in the diocese*. The term 'Vicar of Jesus* Christ*' is also one of the titles of the Pope*.

Vicar forane (Latin *foras* – outside *sc.* the town) Also known as the 'dean*' or 'archpriest*'. A priest* in charge of a group of parish priests* or 'deanery*'.

Vicar general A priest* who assists the bishop* in the governance of the whole diocese*. In some dioceses there may be more than one appointed.

Vice-officialis The assistant to the judicial vicar*.

Visitation The formal visit of a bishop*, or his delegate, to a parish*, to receive an account of the work of the parish. In religious* orders*, individual houses are subject to regular visitation by a senior member of the order for the same purpose.

CANON LAW ON MARRIAGE

The law of the Church* touches most Catholics*, and others, particularly in the field of marriage. This section outlines the canonical requirements in preparing and celebrating a wedding, and the procedures adopted under Canon Law* in the event of a divorced Catholic wishing to marry again in the Church.

When a couple decide to marry, Canon Law requires that they undergo a period of preparation. For this to take place, many dioceses* require that adequate notice (usually a period of six months) is given.

Preparation consists in establishing that both parties are free to marry and whether or not they are baptised, and obtaining the other details that are to be entered in the civil and church marriage registers.* Any necessary dispensations* are sought at this time. Pastoral* preparation is also given, to enable the couple to make the promises and undertake the obligations of Christian* marriage freely and with full understanding. The couple will normally meet with the priest* and others several times to ensure all this is done.

The marriage must be celebrated before the parish priest* or a minister* delegated by him, and must be entered in the parish* marriage register* as well as the civil register. Notification should also be sent to the churches where the parties were baptised, to be entered in their baptism* register.

Certain circumstances render a person unable to marry validly. These are known as 'impediments'*.

Annulment* is the term used to describe a decree of nullity* – an act by which the Church declares that a marriage was invalid from the beginning. The decree will be issued by the diocesan bishop*. Annulment differs from divorce, because it is a declaration that no effectual marriage took place, even though the partners uttered the words of the marriage vows.

A decree of nullity rests on the finding that the promises and the consent exchanged at the wedding were defective, i.e., that they did not represent the true state of mind of one or other partner. If either partner was unable or unwilling to fulfil the responsibilities of marriage, or if they made their assent conditional, then proof of this will mean that an annulment may be given.

The process of establishing this lack of true or full consent is the work of a church court, known as the marriage tribunal*. Most dioceses have their own tribunal. Decisions taken in the diocesan tribunal must be confirmed by an appeal tribunal, usually that belonging to the archdiocese* in whose province* the first tribunal is located. If there is a need to take the case further, it has to go to the Holy See*, to the Roman Rota*, for a third judgement.

The tribunal is a court, though it will not normally meet in formal session.

Witnesses normally testify on oath concerning the partners at the time of their marriage. The evidence must be examined by the defender of the bond* who must propose any reasons why nullity should not be given. After considering the matter the judge will rule in favour of a nullity, or against. Judgements in favour will then proceed to the provincial tribunal where they may be ratified, or further evidence sought.

Affinity (Latin *affinis* – neighbouring, connected) The relationship created by a valid* marriage*. See also **Degrees of affinity**

Annulment The name given to the decree of nullity* establishing that a valid* marriage* was not contracted.

Appeal tribunal The court which reviews and may confirm a nullity* already granted in the diocesan tribunal*.

Banns (Middle English *ban* – proclamation) The public notice given of two people's intention to marry. Banns are not usually used in the Catholic* Church*.

Canonical form See **Form of marriage**

Consanguinity (Latin prefix *con* – with, and *sanguis* – blood) Blood relationship. Such a relationship, if within certain degrees of kinship, is an impediment* to marriage*.

Consent For a marriage* to be valid*, both husband and wife must give their full and free consent, which must be both verbal and psychological. This consent, which constitutes the marriage, is expressed and effected by the promises made at the marriage service.

Consummated (Latin *consummare* – to complete) Sexual intercourse between spouses is said to consummate the marriage*.

Defect (Latin *deficio* – to lack) A circumstance or state of mind that prevents the marriage* being valid*. Defect may be either in the intentions of the spouses, or in the fact that, if Catholics*, they have been married according to a service* other than that of the Catholic Church* and have not received a dispensation* for this to happen.

Defender of the bond The official of the diocesan marriage* tribunal* who examines evidence in nullity* cases to review the arguments against a nullity decree being given.

Degrees of affinity (Latin *affinare* – neighbouring) Family relationships within which marriage* is prohibited by Scripture* and the Church*. See also **Affinity** and **Consanguinity**.

Disparity of worship If a baptised Catholic* wishes to marry someone who is not baptised, then a case of disparity of worship* exists. The bishop* may give a dispensation* to ensure the validity* of the marriage*.

Dispensation (Latin *dispensatio* – relaxation) The permission granted by the diocesan bishop* to allow a marriage*, despite the existence of some impediment*.

Divorce, Church and civil The Church* holds that marriage* when properly entered into, is not able to be dissolved by anyone. Civil divorce, therefore, is not recognised and those divorced are not able to marry again in a Catholic* church* while their spouse is alive, unless an annulment* of the marriage has been possible.

Form of marriage The Rite* of Marriage according to the Catholic* Church*. For a Catholic* to marry validly, they must do so in the presence of the parish priest* or another delegated by him, and in the presence of two witnesses. The Marriage* Rite of the Church must be used, though the bishop* may, for good reason, give a dispensation*, known as a dispensation from canonical form*.

Impediment (Latin *impedimentum* – an obstacle) Factors preventing validity* in a marriage*. Impediments arise through a number of causes: absolute impotence, marriage before canonical age, a previous marriage with a partner still living, marriage between a Catholic* and an unbaptised person. Ordained* ministers* are unable to marry validly, unless dispensed*. Marriages entered into as a result of abduction or the murder of a previous spouse are invalid, as are those between certain degrees of kinship, including adoption. Some of these impediments may be removed by dispensation*.

Marriage tribunal The diocesan court where nullity* cases are processed.

Metropolitan tribunal (Greek *meter* – mother, *polis* – city, and Latin *tribunal* – court) A court sitting in an archdiocese*.

Mixed marriage A marriage between a baptised Catholic* and a baptised person of another Christian* tradition*.

Nullity (Latin *nullus* – none) The decree stating that owing to certain conditions present at the time of the marriage*, the marriage is not valid*.

Pauline privilege Based on 1 Corinthians* 7:12–15, this process enables the diocesan bishop* to dissolve a marriage* between two unbaptised* people following the baptism* of one of them and where also the other person leaves the marriage. This allows the newly baptised person to marry in church*. The 'privilege' becomes effective with the new marriage consent.

Petrine privilege This 'privilege of the faith*' is an extension of the Pauline privilege*. It can be invoked where only one of the parties in a marriage* is not baptised, to allow marriage and to work in favour of the Catholic* faith of either party to the new marriage. This privilege is granted by the Holy See* and becomes effective with the new marriage consent.

Putative A term used to denote a marriage which is annulled, and which was thought at the time to have been valid*. The term allows the children of such a marriage* to remain legitimate.

Ratified A term used to describe a marriage* that has taken place according to the proper form of marriage*.

Validation (Latin *valere* – to be valid) The procedure by which a marriage* which is invalid by reason of an impediment* is made valid*. The marriage consent must be made afresh and the couple must desire to remain together.

Validity The state of a marriage* entered into with the right freedom and dispositions of mind.